£10 -

the new furniture

trends+traditions

PETER DORMER

the new furniture

trends+traditions

With 252 illustrations, 96 in colour

THAMES AND HUDSON

Phototypeset in Great Britain by Keyspools Ltd, Golborne, Lancs
Printed and bound in Japan

CONTENTS

Design for a floor-to-ceiling
adjustable lamp.
Peter Wheeler. UK, 1986

1

INTRODUCTION

Table. Le Corbusier and Charlotte Perriand. Black-enamelled steel and glass.
France, 1928–29. Currently manufactured by Cassina, Italy

Mies, modernism and the moon . . . and back again

Nearly all designers, it seems, are attracted to designing a piece of furniture. Architects are convinced that the chair is architecture writ small; industrial designers are intrigued by the problem of combining mass-manufacture, modern materials, new technology and good looks in a field which, unlike that of other consumer durables, has in the past resisted change; and men and women who would previously have become fine artists have adopted furniture as a medium for self-expression and comment. No one could pretend that all this has happened suddenly, but the pace of change has quickened and the diversity has become increasingly striking in the 1980s. Furniture design has become fascinatingly complex: sometimes it makes sense, sometimes it seems perverse, but always it is interesting.

Furniture design is not a single category: consequently, this book is divided into three parts – domestic furniture; contract furniture; 'one-off' – unique – designs and hand-craft furniture. Even so, all debate about 20th-century design and aesthetics centres upon the modern movement: the arguments may wander off into post-modernism or, more recently, neo-modernism, but at the heart of our speculative activity is this thing we call 'modern'. The modern movement in furniture includes Frank Lloyd Wright, Gerrit Rietveld, Marcel Breuer, Ludwig Mies van der Rohe, and Le Corbusier and Charlotte Perriand (although until comparatively recently her contribution has been overshadowed by her partnership with Le Corbusier). Together they set a standard against which the rest of 20th-century furniture design competes or has to nod towards with obeisance. What is this modern movement?

The German historian and sociologist Jürgen Habermas has said that the word 'modern' was first used (in Latin) in the late 5th century. Thereafter the term reappears throughout European history whenever society seeks to see itself as moving from the old to the new. The concept of progress is intrinsic to modernism, but intrinsic to the concept of progress (at least since the first industrial revolution of the late 18th century) is applied science.

The first industrial revolution flourished in Britain, which led the world in applying technology to production. For the major part of the 19th century Britain was especially proud of its engineering successes, but by the end of the century it was being challenged by France and overtaken by Germany and the United States. The lesson of the second industrial revolution was that applied science gave you the edge; hence the industrial impetus passed to Germany and the USA, the two nations which came to grips with the new technologies, such as electricity and electronics. And it is these two nations that succoured modernism as their technological dominance increased. For example, several design historians have pointed to the strong lead in industrial design provided by the partnership between the German designer Peter Behrens and the huge German electrical engineering combine AEG. Behrens became an adviser to AEG in 1907.

We can simplify things and say that the Germans 'invented' industrial design and the Americans 'invented' mass production, and then the two countries copied each other. Both countries, like Britain, had their rebels who, like Britain's William Morris, were shocked by the brutalizing side of progress. Throughout the 20th century significant numbers of middle-class individuals have favoured a handicrafts or art-craft based approach to manufacturing and their efforts have from time-to-time fed back into mainstream design interests throughout the West. However, it was largely in Britain that intellectuals, aided by an anti-scientific education system, sought to resist progress and modern industrial design. And even the best of British designers have, until recently, had an arts-and-crafts sympathy somewhere in their philosophy: indeed, this has sometimes proved to be their strength.

There is a difference between modernism as the spirit of progress inventing and applying technology, and the modern movement as an aesthetic expression of that progress. The spirit of modernism was alive and thrusting in AEG in Germany well before Peter Behrens cleaned it up aesthetically and turned its electrical goods (whether deliberately or not) into symbols as well as models of progress. Making a new thing look modern usually occurs some time after its first appearance in the market place. Most new technology is introduced in the guise of the old.

The response in 19th-century America to the demand for furniture from large numbers of people setting up new homes was to industrialize the furniture industry – a process well under way by the 1840s. For a long time the designs were frequently kitsch versions of the half-remembered styles from old Europe. Nevertheless, by the end of the 19th century the American furniture industry was industrial in a way quite unknown in Europe, although Germany was learning fast about modern production methods.

John Kouwenhoven, author of *Made in America* (1948), says that modernism was 'an American secret' hidden in the new factories, the new cities and the hustle and bustle of commerce and manufacturing – of the 19th century. The dominant principle of mass manufacturing had been practised, if not perfected, by the slaughterhouses and meat-packing stations in the mid-1840s. West Germany apart, most of Europe did not catch up with America's modern age until the early 1960s. Britain's car industry did not manage it until the early 1980s.

In terms of a modern movement aesthetic, however, it was Europe, not America, that generally led the way. But even in Europe, designers in the modern movement had a hard time trying to bounce manufacturers out of their habit of introducing new inventions – and new materials – in old forms. With hindsight, we can see that the crucial rupture with aesthetic tradition, which helped greatly to launch the modern movement as an aesthetic force, was made by the work of two Dutchmen – Piet Mondrian, with his paintings, and Gerrit Rietveld, with his infamous Red and Blue chair of 1918. The Red and Blue chair is one of the emblems of the modern movement. No doubt, being handmade and a product of traditional carpentry, it is less significant a modernist breakthrough than Ford's Model T, but as an intellectual break with historicism it presented a denouement in the process of regarding furniture as architecture – a process which had begun before the First World War with the radical work of the American architect Frank Lloyd Wright, to whom Rietveld was surely indebted.

There was also the influence of the Bauhaus. Once it had got over its initial indebtedness to handicraft, it became one of the key intellectual centres of the modern movement, even though few of its designs went into the mass production for which they were intended.

Reyner Banham, design historian and philosopher, points out that at first the modernists at the Bauhaus had technical innovations, such as cantilevers and glass walling in architecture (and metal bending and fabrication techniques in furniture), but no aesthetic discipline to bind everything together. That aesthetic came from abstract art, especially the theoretical and conceptual work of the Futurists, the De Stijl group, and the Russian Constructivists. All European ideas, not American.

The ideologies that Europe forged between the two World Wars were audacious in their predictions. On the one hand, there were Piet Mondrian's utopian manifestos, a typical opening sentence of which – more wishful thinking than fact – was: 'The life of modern cultured man is generally turning away from the natural: it is becoming more and more abstract.' On the other hand, scientists were also saying their piece. One of the more extraordinary documents is *The World, the Flesh and the Devil* by the English physicist J. D. Bernal, published in 1929. The first part is a straightforward discussion of man's inorganic environment, and how this could be improved through physical alteration and faith in the machine. But it is what Bernal has to say about the future of man himself and the predicted alterations to the human flesh that is particularly 'unreal'. Bernal predicted that eventually the body would be dispensed with and that the brains of people would be connected via machines. He wrote: 'And if this seems only a way of cheating death, we must realize that the individual brain will feel itself part of the whole in a way that completely transcends the devotion of the most fanatical adherent of a religious sect.'

Ideologically, several people in the modern movement were led towards the communal. Bernal's expression of it is only extreme in retrospect for, as the Italian architect and philosopher

Left, The Brno chair. Mies van der Rohe. High-tensile flat steel with polished chrome finish, leather-cased foam cushioning. Germany, 1929–30. Currently manufactured by Knoll International, USA

Right, The Landi stacking chair. Hans Coray. Aluminium. Switzerland, 1939. Currently manufactured by Zanotta, Italy

about design, Andrea Branzi, says – between the two World Wars Rationalism, Fascism, Nazism and Soviet Socialism all proposed something no other ideology had ever done: the modification of the human race. Until then modification had been left to God through the concept of redemption.

America, too, had its ideology for transforming men and women: Frederick Winslow Taylor had published in America a book called *The Principles of Scientific Management* (1911): this book (the subject of a special Congressional investigating committee in 1912) argued the principles for making a labour force efficient and in tune with the production lines – it aimed to remove hit-or-miss attitudes in planning. After the First World War this book caught on in Europe. And what seemed to awe intellectuals and politicians alike was not just the machine, but the workers' relationship to it.

Understandably, artists and designers rather romanticized the machine age. As an aesthetic movement, the modern movement has been caricatured as thoroughly non-emotional. But this is misleading. As Reyner Banham observes: 'Emotion had played a much larger part than logic in the creation of the style; inexpensive buildings had been clothed in it, but it was no more an inherently economical style than any other. The true aim of the style had clearly been about the Bauhaus and its relation to the world of the machine age ... to invent and create forms symbolising that world.'

In its idealism the modern movement may have affected some of its protagonists like a quasi-religious movement. It parallels, in its intensity and some of its aims, the technological and utilitarian progress made by the 19th-century American Shakers. This movement, as a by-product, produced an aesthetic that modernists admire. The irony is, however, that the Shakers were not seeking beauty (a frivolity), but truth.

The Shakers were puritans and their Christianity, like the modern movement's belief in rationality and the harmony of abstract formal relations, was also based on notions of harmony and regularity. Shakers attempted to create a material world that was not only without error but revealed harmony in all its aspects. Among the written declarations of the Shakers is this: 'There is great beauty in harmony. Order is the creation of beauty. It is heaven's first law, and the protection of souls.'

The Shakers demonstrated how a shared, coherent value system, operating essentially from a spirit of good will, resulted in design of beauty and universality even though neither style nor beauty were their goals. Beauty came from truth and truth was fitness for purpose: good design, though not a goal in itself, was a result of this philosophy.

Similarly, the modernist movement attempted to construct an ideology which would frame values, provide objectives and ban doubt, confusion and scepticism. It, too, used functionalism as the justification for a reductivist design approach; it eschewed ornament, and was intent on revealing structure because that way there could be no dishonesty. That, at any rate, is the acceptable myth of the modern movement which, even had it not existed, would need to have been invented as a necessary ideal for designers to work towards.

Hardly surprisingly, the focus of much modern movement attention was the working class. In Austria, Germany and Holland, and later in Britain, the working class presented an excellent (and powerless) target for the new puritanism in worker housing design and fittings for that housing. Vienna, Frankfurt, Berlin and Weimar were among the pioneering cities to provide worker housing in the modern idiom. Such housing needed the appropriate furniture. Workers were intimate with machines, workers were therefore radical, workers were not middle class; therefore the appropriate design for them was honest modern movement design without the fripperies of the bourgeoisie. Functionalism seemed suited to workers.

However, functionalism was frequently set aside by early modern movement designers because, ironically, the modern world for which the European modernists were designing was much more complicated and demanding than that of a simple abstract universe envisaged by the head-in-the-sky painters of the De Stijl group. Modernism's harmony of verticals, horizontals and planes did not necessarily result in functional boxes.

In his *Modern Movement in Architecture* (1973) the American architect Charles Jencks explains that in such buildings by Mies van der Rohe as Farnsworth House, the beauty of the ideal form is possible only by compromising the function of the building; and in describing the Crown Hall Illinois Institute of Technology in Chicago, he observes: 'Mies for instance, makes wonderful buildings only because he ignores many aspects of a building. If he solved more problems his buildings would be far less potent.' Sometimes the same was true of his furniture, as the irreverent journalist Tom Wolfe noted in *From Bauhaus to Our House* (1981): 'Mies van der Rohe's S shaped, tubular steel, cane bottomed chairs were designed so that by the time the main course arrived, at least one guest had pitched face forward into the lobster bisque.'

But this is unduly negative. The good thing about the modern movement was that it at least had an aesthetic value system and as a result it laid down some fundamental rules of beauty in design. And comfort. Mies van der Rohe's justifiably famous Barcelona chair is one of the classics of 20th-century design; it looks beautiful and it is very comfortable. Other modernists designing between the wars, such as Le Corbusier, Perriand and Eileen Gray, produced works of grace and practicality.

The imagery of plane and line, rudely punched home by Rietveld, was made poetic by Marcel Breuer with his Wassily bent tubular steel chair with caning, and his later, cantilever tubular steel chair with caning which has been much copied and is very popular with people who seek the 'modern' image for their dining rooms.

Constraints, even the artificial ones of an aesthetic theory, can achieve good results. For instance, curator and writer Ludwig Glaeser explains that the modernists implicitly rejected upholstery (presumably because it looked old-fashioned, middle class, conservative and anti-architectural — a full-blown sofa looks like a stranded whale, not a platonically ideal piece of geometry.) Glaeser writes: 'Like all designers of modern furniture in the 1920s and 1930s Mies constantly sought an acceptable substitute for the bulky spring elements in conventional upholstered chairs, which had fallen under the modernist ban; reduced as they were to minimal components, the new chairs seemed to offer but one option to improve their comfort and that was through flexibility built into the steel support frames or wooden seat shells themselves. The search for resilience, however, lost its urgency with the introduction of foam rubber as a compact upholstery material but this was not used extensively until after the 2nd world war.'

In the late 1920s, at the height of the modern movement's first flush, the orthodoxy of having to express the idea of the machine metaphorically in all one's designs was rigid. Charlotte Perriand explains: 'Naturally, I made myself a necklace of ball-bearing, a cocktail bar in sheet aluminium with chairs of chrome tube, an extendable table with a rubber top — everything except that produced by the furniture trade. I was not interested in timber, I was ill at ease with it, it didn't fit my ethic which was concerned with mechanical objects . . . I promoted metal — its potential for perfect triangulated jointing, the escape it offered from complicated joinery and fussiness . . . I contrasted it with timber, which perishes, expands, contracts, dries out.' But later she dropped her materials index. 'I learnt that there are no unusable materials … I saw shepherds make small seats from odd bits of wood, anything that came to hand. I asked myself, what is wrong with that? It is appropriate to their environment, the ecology, their economy and it meets their needs. The value was obvious.'

The Second World War inevitably redirected the modern movement and many European architects and designers emigrated to America. Abstraction lost its metaphysical discipline and in New York even Piet Mondrian loosened up and started painting boogie woogies. And eventually the traffic between Europe and America became two-way. An Italian perspective on what happened is given by Andrea Branzi: 'With the Allies landing at Anzio, American industry was disembarking the "new man" of another, simpler more brutal but clearly winning ideology, an ideology in which immediate happiness was seen as the only possible foundation for human society, but a real society in which industry was expected to provide health, abundance, surplus and consumer goods.'

After the Second World War America took an important lead in future design. Two companies, Herman Miller and Knoll International, were prominent in turning the modern movement in furniture design into what is better called the 'International' style and sold it all over the industrialized world. Knoll International firmly established its links with the modern movement by producing (and indeed improving) a range of Mies van der Rohe designs. The modern aesthetic fitted in well with the corporate identity philosophy of the business world (note the Morrison office system discussed in Chapter 3).

The best-known furniture designers of the 1950s and early 1960s (excepting Van der Rohe, Breuer, Aalto) were Eero Saarinen and Charles Eames. Eames designed for Herman Miller, Saarinen for Knoll. Penny Sparke in *Furniture* (1986) notes that by the mid-1950s modern furniture had become accepted by a large section of America's mass market. She also points out that the 'modern style' gained acceptance there first by appearing in public places such as cocktail bars and hotel foyers, and entered the home via the kitchen. But work like Saarinen's became more widely popular than that of the orthodox modernists because it was organic. In America there is a considerable liking for well-rounded, organic shapes – they seem to be a visual metaphor for the good life. Saarinen's designs became a cliché and mass-manufacturers copied them profitably.

Reyner Banham says that the modern movement ended around 1970. Perhaps this is poetic licence, but if Banham is right then it is a nice point that this should have coincided with landing men on the moon, which first happened in 1969. It completes the circle and fulfils at least one of the modernist visions as described by J. D. Bernal: space travel, he asserted, was a logical aspiration of the machine age. Bernal thus described a form of space travel that he called 'space sailing'. 'A space vessel spreading its large, metallic wings, acres in extent, to the full, might be

Left, Womb chair and foot stool. Eero Saarinen for Knoll International. Moulded plastic seat, steel frame, foam cushioning. USA, 1948

Right, Pedestal chair. Eero Saarinen for Knoll International. Moulded plastic (seat) and steel (base). USA, 1956

blown to the limit of Neptune's orbit. Then to increase its speed, it would tack, close hauled, down the gravitational field, spreading full sail again as it rushed past the sun.'

After 1970 did the modern movement crash, Icarus-like? Perhaps. It has been argued that the modern movement was a victim of its own success: it was everywhere, so people grew bored with it. That may be true of architecture, but then the International Style in architecture was subverted by financial expediency which turned architecture into boxes of air-conditioning units. More important, the modern movement had supplied the visual metaphors for progress, but in the 1970s there was a loss of faith in progress. Science was suspect because each of its benefits possessed a negative: even medicine and agriculture had their human or environmental cost. Political science was suspect, too: the models for social engineering in housing, health and social integration so assiduously applied in the 1950s and 1960s (and with political consensus) went askew.

In any case, in some areas, especially the living room of the home, the modern movement was always regarded with unease. If Main Street stores are a guide, then the majority of homes in the majority of Western countries are wary of the modern style. Even in design-conscious countries such as Italy, Germany and Holland working-class and bourgeois taste moves sluggishly around a pudding of heavy solid woodenness: four layers of treacle-type varnish over a plywood base adds up to perceived gravitas. Generalized old-fashionedness is popular.

By 1980 post-modernism was the fashionable style and its logic was impeccable. Since we only like what we already know (if we are unfamiliar with something we are not able to say with certainty that we like it), it follows that if both architecture and furniture are to be liked then both have to be historical – to quote from the past. In order to be familiar to us post-modernist stylists dip into classical furniture and sweep in and out of the Baroque, they fish in the Nile for Ancient Egypt and slum a little in 20th-century kitsch. For evidence of this tendency in its most extreme state, look at Chapter 4, which shows a selection of American post-modern 'art-craft' furniture. A less extreme example is the furniture of Michael Graves, doyen architect of the American 1980s, whose work looks distinctly 1930s. 148, 150

Of the several leading characters in the post-modernist story, four have designed furniture and all are architects. Robert Venturi, Andrea Branzi, Michael Graves and Charles Jencks. Robert Venturi, who demonstrated his percipience by publishing in 1966 his seminal *Complexity and Contradiction in Architecture*, in many ways remains a modernist. Venturi's book approached the problem of the predictability of the International Style by arguing the need for some ornament which had coherence and a content. He did not support irrationality. He has introduced for our inspection a range of ornamental, post-modernist chairs which are worth consideration alongside those of a fellow American who has followed in his theoretical wake, Charles Jencks.

Venturi's range of ornate bentwood chairs for Knoll International and his gorgeous stuffed 46–48 sofas were launched in 1984 and they are now famous. Several critics have written about the interplay in Venturi's furniture between Marcel Breuer, Alvo Aalto, Chippendale and Hepplewhite. He told me: 'I have always been fascinated by chairs and furniture and even as a kid I knew the difference between a Hepplewhite and a Queen Anne. I drew a bunch of bentwood chairs one weekend: they fitted my architecture. And then I approached Knoll.'

The Venturi bentwood chairs look like modernist chairs in profile, but full frontal they are ornate and elaborate, and also deliberately artificial like stage sets. They are pieces of theatre but in addition intellectual plays on the nature of illusion and representation. 'I am very interested in the representation of a chair by its profile – like a Victorian theatre cut-out. I am interested in the representation of full form rather than its actuality.' The very local context for Venturi's work might be Philadelphia, where he works. In south Philadelphia, in the Italian quarter, the fancied up façades have the flat decorative quality of his chairs.

What criteria does he use for judging his furniture design? 'It is successful when all the ingredients come together as a whole – but this does not necessarily mean they have to be in balance. The chair might be skewed in some way but still be a great chair. The whole consists of the rational and the emotional though they may be in unequal proportions.'

He comments on the context in which he works: 'I am interested in form and symbol, but not the opportunism of post-modernism. In the beginning I came to ornament rationally – I acknowledged the importance of ornament but I did not know what to say – I was working from no context. I think of myself as pretty rational. I grew up on space and form. I spent four years designing one building [he did a house for his mother].' But he admits: 'Ornament I'll never really get because I came to it too late and I mistrust being historically referential. I don't want to be too esoteric. Historicism stinks – people don't have the background to understand it.'

An objection to Venturi's assertion about historical reference might be that people can still enjoy a work without understanding its pedigree. Yet uncritical quotation by designers of past styles leads to genteel kitsch and since no one has the knowledge to challenge what the designers are doing, the kitsch sticks – it gets taken for the thing itself. This has happened in the applied arts. In the craft revivals after the last World War much quasi-Oriental furniture has been made in England and the USA. It looks Korean or Chinese so long as you do not compare it with the source material: then you begin to notice the inadaquacy of – not the construction – but the balance and composition of the parts.

In practical terms, of course, there can be no hard rules about using history. Since each designer (unless he or she is a fool) learns from his peers and from the past what has already been achieved and what is possible, then in a sense history is not only inevitable but desirable. By the same token, a part of the argument of this book is that designers should not dismiss the modern movement in their haste to be fashionable.

The challenge Venturi so rightly raised years ago was to remind designers that decoration was not a sin against progress but an important part of man's visual tradition, and one that people enjoyed. Yet making contemporary decoration is not easy. In the past there was a common visual vocabulary which was rooted in Christianity and the land. But in an urban and largely secular society such imagery does not make much sense. So the problem is: what can the contemporary designer use by way of decoration that other people can share in? One could envisage a kind of pop-art imagery devised from current advertising, but how many people want a decorative order in their homes based on the clowning of Ronald McDonald (of McDonald's burger fame)? Interestingly, Antonia Astori (Italy) makes a sophisticated attempt at this in Chapter 2.

Charles Jencks has had an honourable go at developing a style of complexity and coherence in the furniture he designed for his London house, documented in his book *Symbolic Architecture* (1985). The rooms on the ground floor have been organized according to the four seasons – the 'seasons' are the most popular organizing metaphor in contemporary applied arts because, unlike recondite religious, mythological or literary imagery, they are easy on the brain and also allow very general symbolism that deals with growth, darkness to light, seed to harvest, balance between masculine and feminine. In fact in Jencks' house there is an interesting mixture of the obvious and the recondite, an understandable combination given that Jencks himself appears to want to be both reassured and stimulated by his surroundings. For example, in the 'Winter' room there are two armchairs described as 'very heavy chairs, portly gentlemen, conferring with two Biedermeiers'.

Possibly the best-known 'image' to come out of this house so far is the Sun chair – a popular image because of its historical attachment to Egyptian style. The Egyptian style is always resurfacing in decorative revivals because people seem to like its mixture of sophistication and childishness, solidity and trumpery.

Jencks has tried to face up to the difficulty of constructing meaning; he has apparently done this by thinking the house through as a landscape for domestic ritual. However, his difficulty – and that of any sensitive designer – is that the business of inventing a decorative order full of references and quotations can end up as an arbitrary mixture. Decorative orders are cussed creatures: they resist invention, they prefer to grow slowly. (Jencks has references ranging from Dutch interior paintings to the philosopher Heraclitus.) The most important quality that a genuinely 'natural' or simply old and familiar decorative order has is its sense of rightness: the Christian cross, the fish, the lily are now inseparable from their meanings. But with post-modernism the demand for content and meaning has been so quick, so sudden, that there has been no opportunity for the passage of time to allow a form to acquire an accepted meaning.

The less ambitious the designer is in seeking to invent a new decorative order of complex meaning, the easier it is for all concerned: Venturi's sofa looks Victorian, looks like homemade jam and looks like an archetype of grandmotherly comfort. It may be tongue in cheek but it is all right, it looks natural: Venturi has given us a well-designed decorative and rather glorious object. His bentwood chairs look very much more contrived. It is not that they are badly designed, far from it. Among the designs that we can characterize as post-modern these are good; they are intelligent, coherent, balanced – they are good conversations. But for all that they suffer from post-modernism's achilles heel, which is to say they lack necessity.

This notion of 'necessity' is elusive. The most unnecessary object in New York is (or was until its example spawned imitators desirous of being more outrageously 'decorative') Philip Johnson's AT&T building with its Chippendale top. But bit by bit it will settle in alongside the equally 'unnecessary' tops of the Empire State and the Chrysler building. It is so easy (and misleading) for the old to simulate gravitas; while we are rightly critical of new design when we suspect it is full of gimmickry, we tend to let the old design alone because the patina of familiarity has protected it against our scepticism. Old politicians with grey hair can spout complete rubbish, but from their venerable lips it has the tone of authority. Similar difficulties occur when trying to assess post-modern designers: they keep dressing up at one and the same time in contemporary party frocks and in the silver-haired wigs of art history.

Most counter movements to the modern movement have been centred on the debate about 'should we decorate or not, and what sort of decoration should it be?' Andrea Branzi's book *The Hot House* (1985) also deals with decoration, but Branzi's philosophical break with modernism is fundamental. In an interview with me, he asserted: 'The previous industrial system made everything well ordered – the philosophy of production was an emphasis on order and unity. Now there is a great vitality in the post-industrial city: free time, spare time – now people try to take their models from a variety of images. According to this philosophy the great mass markets have disappeared and therefore the market has come to mean lots of little markets.' The understanding of the expressive is, says Branzi, one of the most important aspects separating Italian from English [and German] design: 'The soft technology of Italy has worked for the expressive quality of the product together with its technical quality. It is applied technology used to emphasize its expressive qualities. Italian design has always been very unorthodox.'

Branzi may be too hasty in kissing goodbye to the mass-market concept, which is very much alive. Around the world India, North and South Korea, Taiwan, China and other countries are gearing up industrially. Moreover, their intended markets include Europe, from which we may infer that the market for the mass consumer object is not over. Indeed, the concept of the world marketed car (and to a lesser degree, but pertinent to this book, the world office chair) is gaining in commercial credibility. New technology has added the bonus of making dozens of minor variations possible to the same basic product, thus allowing the bulk producer to 'serve the individual' without losing the economy of mass production. New technology favours the large producer as well as the small workshop.

172 Branzi is especially interested in the role that decoration plays in increasing an object's expressive value and in its power for influencing the emotional quality of the environment. He says: 'Nowadays decoration ought to be seen as a system of information in its own right: cultural information about the product and information on its use, as well as linguistic and visual information. 'And he says that emotional expression is made up of 'the object's basic materials, its shape, weight, smell, tactile characteristics and perceptual presence: from high-tech to high touch'. He has sought to put on an intellectual (and therefore overt) footing what millions of 'ordinary' people have understood implicitly: objects can make you feel happy, unhappy, alienated, secure, calm, comforted, agitated, interested, uncomfortable, nauseous, or indifferent.

In the retailing of domestic furniture there has in the last few years been a marked development in presenting furniture in themes – analogous to, though never as erudite, as Charles Jencks' rooms; and with an understanding of the emotional vocabulary less semantically sharp than Branzi's, but nevertheless in the same camp. The difference between modern retailers and Andrea Branzi is that he wants furniture (and other domestic objects) to raise questions; most retailers and their designers believe that most consumers want their furniture to be familiar and reassuring, and to raise no questions at all.

There is one interesting point. Branzi is in love with 'chaos' and he spoke (in 1986) of a project he was working on which 'creates discontinuity within familiar urban surroundings'. This is the antithesis of the commercial attitude in designing and selling furniture. Indeed, in the photographs in the majority of furniture catalogues (be they overtly 'design'-orientated or not) the domestic landscapes thus presented are strangely unpeopled. The chaos of people is avoided: there are no pot bellies, no senile grandparents, sullen adolescents or loudmouth three-year-olds.

Branzi is by no means alone in wanting discontinuity in a landscape where most people want domestic order, comfort and security. Throughout Europe and the USA all manner of designers have taken the chair or the table and made it an object that is frankly subversive of bourgeois attitudes. Chapter 4 has several of these objects. They are made by men and women working outside the mainstream of commerce and either supplying the art galleries or feeding that small market of interested purchasers that commerce cannot afford to serve. There are purchasers who are gifted with curiosity, excited by the very new and willing to live with the tension of having to discover whether or not they like a piece of work. However, Branzi, unlike one or two of the designers whose furniture is pictured in Chapter 4, is not an anarchist. He is a positive creator. He is excited by the new questions that the post-modern era offers, but observes: 'this is a very dangerous period. Designers should meet this new situation by creating places for psychological peace, desirable objects, a desirable world.' (Has such a view anything to do with the revival of interest in the Shakers among Milanese architects?)

Branzi's arguments interest me because he tries intelligently to resolve several post-modern contradictions. We do look to designers for desirable worlds and yet we do not especially demand that they do anything new. On the contrary, the majority of people appear to believe that they either know what is desirable, or find that Main Street provides them with their desirable objects, with peace and with their sanctuaries. There is a huge 20th-century vernacular which is based on generalized old-fashionedness, 'craft' and country living – an amalgam that amounts to a common set of values. Venturi understands the lesson one hundred per cent with his sofas.

Yet so much of what Main Street offers is generalized escapism, short on quality, manifesting a general reactionary stance, a withdrawal into ignorance, the 'comfy', shunning all questions. Consequently, applause must go to the 'radicals' in design for mounting an opposition to ignorance, for at least seeking to counter the reactionary attitudes of escapism. In England, in the Cotswolds, there are little villages where they try to hide the bright red public telephone boxes by painting them grey in order to make them 'disappear' and not remind the good citizens that they are in the 20th century. Similar 'disguise and forget' escapism is rampant in Main Street throughout Western Europe and North America.

But let me finish this chapter by looking at two architect designers whose work is of its time, is questioning, but is also intended to serve people through comfort, durability and, indeed, contemporary beauty. Both designers are modernists: one is the Italian, Anna Castelli Ferrieri; the other, the Austrian, Matteo Thun.

35–38   Ferrieri practises as an architect and as an industrial designer. She has worked closely with Kartell, a company specializing in the manufacture of injection-moulded plastic artefacts, including chairs, tables and storage systems. She is expert in plastics technology and both mindful and proud of the fact that she is one of the very few 'industrial designers' working in furniture in Italy. The industrial designer is a modernist: solving the problem of mass production of objects which have integrity, are affordable and profitable. Ferrieri says: 'I am not a post-modernist. I think to the future. Post-modernism has no answers.'

Plastic is not new to furniture, but to make an armchair entirely in plastic that is light, strong and aesthetic demands advanced engineering. The Kartell stackable chair 4870 has two arms that posed Ferrieri a major problem: how could they be made of a piece with the seat of the chair, but with elegance and sufficient rigidity. The arms of a chair take a lot of stress: when people sit down or get up they use them to support themselves; moreover, people all move slightly differently and not all stresses are predictable. The internal plane of the 4870's arm turns in space like a mobius strip.

The responsibility on the industrial designer is considerable: for example, the capital investment on the 4870 chair was around $700,000, and the company is looking for sales of tens of thousands a year over many years. One of Ferrieri's aesthetic breakthroughs (look also at her range of tables) is to demonstrate that plastic furniture need not be composed of bulky forms.

106, 107   Perversely, Matteo Thun would be appalled to be described as an industrial designer because he associates this term with the market-research, narrowly functionalist school of design based on anal repression. Thun is a modified modernist: he has returned to the machine-led aesthetic via the apotheosis of post-modernism – the Memphis association, whose researches into decoration and counter design peaked in Milan in 1982 under the direction of Ettore Sottsass. Thun says: 'Memphis was important because it was a mental gymnasium. It was important for the redevelopment of decoration. It revitalized surface decoration and made it modern by using the language of modern times. The surface patterns which Memphis generated were continuous, they had no beginning or end. They took their imagery from computer graphics, from machine-made patterns, and dropped all the historical baggage. The other important aspect which Memphis developed was the tactile quality of the object. Giving back a sensation of touch between an object and a person.'

Thun comments: 'I design objects only when I need them for an architectural project. If they are then suitable for mass production then that is good. But first each object I design has a specific purpose.' This is a very important distinction because a product designer works to someone else's brief and above all to a conception of a 'market'. Thun, like an artist, works for himself, but bearing other people in mind because 'I am interested in communication. I am not, however, interested in the Utopia of beauty. I am not interested in the shapes of an object but in what an object communicates. Communication is possible through the modern language of architecture and the machine.'

Thun has designed a cheap metal tray – and 100,000 of them were sold in six months of production. Few of the purchasers will have analysed its architectural language, recognized its post-Memphis pedigree, or understood the language of the machine for which it was designed. None the less, 100,000 people have been beguiled by it. Its desirability factor has been proved empirically.

Thun speaks also of the language of the machine. This is demonstrated by Bieffeplast, who are manufacturing a sheet metal storage system designed by Thun. He explains that the various proportions of the parts were determined by the abilities of the machine – the possibilities of a machine and its limitations provide its vocabulary. Thun's interest in using modern automated lathe technology is unbounded and follows from his own version of 'Utopia', which is to produce material things that will bring pleasure to people as cheaply as possible. 'But,' he says, 'I am not talking about form following function.' Memphis is the key to his new rapport with modernism: it led to a synthesis of opposites in his mind – the Bauhaus with the Baroque.

In their different but equally rationalist ways both Thun and Ferrieri demonstrate the direction in which design is going: making use of advanced thinking to serve people with a contemporary but non-subversive design. It will have a courteous charm. But it will also reflect the day-to-day visual appearances of contemporary life – it will take, it does take, the surface marks of modern materials, city scapes and electronic technology and turn them into a non-nostalgic abstract decoration. Thereby it humanizes objects made by machines without the interference of, or reference to, handicraft. It amounts to a rejection of the pessimism of post-modernism and a re-affirmation of belief in progress in applied science. Some may argue that this is itself a sentimental reiteration of 19th-century propaganda. On the contrary, it is simply faith in our ability to use design and applied science to better our material existence, whilst acknowledging that other quasi-design activities – such as applied art and handicraft – also have an important role, tempering hard design with more fanciful delight and solace.

2

THE ARMCHAIR AS HERO

Diamond chair. Harry Bertoia for Knoll International. Steel. Italy/USA, 1952

Furniture design
in the domestic landscape

As soon as the Second World War was over, people wanted to begin making new homes. As early as 1946, for example, advertisements were appearing in Britain under such headlines as 'For the modern home – available now'; and there would be a picture of the new domestic furniture. Its characteristics were lightness and simplicity. By the end of the 1950s there was an international domestic style – a simple geometry of thin legs, thin planes and rounded seats. Bulk was out. Italy and Scandinavia provided the basic lightness of touch in this design. New industry, especially the aircraft makers and the petro-chemical engineering companies, provided the materials and techniques: plywood bending, sheet metal working, plastic moulding, plastic and fibreglass shells, improvements in foam rubber (which meant a revolution in upholstery) and the creation of a synthetic and clean environment.

The new look expressed the fresh start. The popularity of Scandinavian design for twenty years after the War was bound in with its simple, craft style – a good metaphor for decent, clean and reliable domesticity. The new look was also determined by costs and by the smaller size of the new homes. Some kinds of furniture fell into disfavour – free-standing kitchen cabinets gave way to built-in cupboards, as did wardrobes, dressers and china cabinets. The mass furniture market also became intensely price competitive. In the USA and West Germany, from the mid-1950s onwards, the furniture industries were improved by rationalization and investment in new machinery, but the situation in other countries was different. Italy continued with its tradition of being a small-business, artisan-based economy (which some people argue gave – and gives – it the advantage of flexibility, diversity of skill and low costs). Britain's modernization has been piecemeal. After the War international trade in furniture was led by Denmark, Sweden and Finland and this, together with the relative simplicity (and therefore ease of mass manufacture) of their furniture, encouraged the modern industrialization of their factories. However, in the 1970s the introduction of computer-operated lathes, routers and cutting machines helped countries as diverse as Yugoslavia, Belgium and Taiwan to dominate the international market with cheap, mass-produced furniture made in almost any style you want. The only area of furniture that is not especially prominent in international trade today is upholstered goods, because these are bulky and therefore expensive to transport.

Throughout the West the domestic market has stratified in terms of price and value for

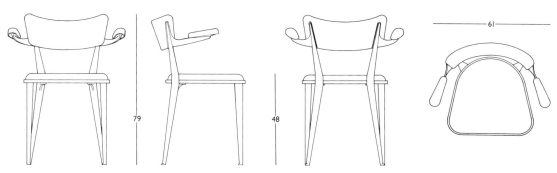

BA 3 chair. Ernest Race. Aluminium. UK, 1945

money. The biggest development, successful in North America and Britain, has been in the lower quality category of the mass market, where price competitiveness has encouraged the science of low-cost substitution. Leather, wood, cloth, good-quality chromium-plated steel – still the basic materials for well-engineered furniture – all have their mass-market ghosts in plastic veneers, nylon fabrics and vinyl. The same is true for design styles. Like the clothing industry and its relationship to the design-led fashion houses, the mass-market furniture industry copies design innovations, but at a much lower quality and, it must be said, less frequently.

The relationship between design-led furniture and marketing-led furniture is tentative but important. Design-led furniture is possible because generally it is made from good materials and sold as a status object to a small but wealthy clientele. If such work looks as though it can be made popular, then the bigger manufacturer will pick it up – maybe a decade after it first emerges. West Germany, Italy and Scandinavia remain the countries where design innovation will find a relatively wide public.

Designers, as critic Deyan Sudjic argues in *The International Design Yearbook 1986/87*, have become like pop stars. Since the 1960s the stars have tended to be Italian, although perhaps none has risen so quickly to public attention as the French designer, Philippe Starck. Starck was helped by the publicity he received when he was commissioned by President Mitterand to design the furnishings of his private apartment in the Elysée Palace. His work alludes to pre-Second World War chic and it is a continuous metaphor for status – it recalls the ages of gracious, servant-saturated travel, whether by ship, rail or airship, in the 1920s and 1930s. And since relatively few of us were alive then, our liking for Starck's work is laced with nostalgia which is fed through old photographs and posters.

Starck is probably too avant-garde for Main Street, too close, in fact, to the aesthetic of the machine. It is true that homes with a traditional living room and a technologically sophisticated

13–15
19–21
57

or futuristic kitchen are not unusual. However, wherever the kitchen is treated as the hub of the house, as the place where the family spends its day-to-day life, then technology is played down; natural materials such as wood and quarry tiling predominate over vinyl and steel. Moreover, no amount of designer-led marketing will convince people that a chair is a body tool, or a table a food facilitator.

Things that are close to the body must be physically close and mentally comfortable. In the living room Robert Venturi's sofa is a natural hero. We know this for fact because Main Street tells us so. Both comfort and perceived craftsmanship are essentials in home furnishing and Scandinavian designers have reflected both in a language of light woods, and soft but not overly organic forms. The Scandinavian countries are noted for their welfare states, social engineering and social responsibility, and they have an interest in designing total environments that are intended to suit everyone.

Two Norwegian designers have developed a systems approach to the living room. Svein   18
Asbjørnsen and Jan Lade explain: 'During the course of a day the living room in a home is a central place. It must serve a variety of functions and people, and is the focal point for social contact. The furniture should stimulate and inspire further activity.' Their 'furniture for flexibility' system includes a settee on which you can sleep, a 'cosy corner', a nest table to use across your lap when you need it, and a combination table that adjusts either as a writing desk or dining table. All the seats are adjustable for different postures. The special feature in this furniture is the use of a 'split' in the upright or horizontal planes of the seating. This allows you to pull and adjust the pillows, head and back rests along the length of the seat or chaise longue, thereby creating a configuration that suits your body. The designs are conservatively modern.

The Danes in particular have stayed true to good modern design by using serviceable materials that are used without trickery: if plastics are used, they are generally used in their own right, not as fake wood or marble. Danish designers have found a middlebrow and affordable – but not cut-price – aesthetic. It does not play on consumer ignorance by being a pastiche of an older style, nor impose too much on the consumer's security by being too radical. The Danish designers Rud Thygesen and Johnny Sorensen confirm that it is possible to design well, make   58, 59
well, sell well and make lots of money with integrity.

Thygesen and Sorensen design domestic and office furniture, constructed in wood, usually beech, with a combination of automated machinery and hand-finishing. Their work does not change radically from year to year; it is thoughtful but not proselytizing. The design process is underpinned by thorough prototyping and close liaison with production engineers.

The development of the conservative modern look has progressed in Europe partly through the efforts of individual designers and partly through enterprising marketing by large value-for-money stores such as IKEA (Scandinavia) and Habitat (UK). However, every style, including that of the restrained modernist or soft modernist, has its leading practitioners. And apart from Thygesen and Sorensen, Ronald Carter (UK) and Gijs Bakker (Holland) are important.

2–5   Bakker is an unusually diverse designer. He was known in the early 1970s for his radical
68–71 innovations in jewelry (see *The New Jewelry*, 1985), but he also practises industrial design. Bakker's furniture follows, naturally, from his interest in body sculpture and jewelry (because of the relationship between form and the human body), but his furniture designs — though contemporary — are mainstream in their aesthetic. They exist to give pleasure — they reflect a Dutchman's instinct for good-quality democratic design. Bakker occasionally uses combinations of metal and wood, but the vitality in his work lies less in contrast between materials than in the dynamism of the line. In a succession of designs, which includes the Strip, Torsion, Webbing and Finger chairs, we see the language of engineering and practical physics played off against his pleasure in making abstract compositions. The engineering metaphor is exciting and as often as not a Bakker chair spans space like the leap of a bridge. To a degree, Bakker has outshone the Danes, whose reticence has verged a little on the dull. Bakker demonstrates a difference between soft and flabby modernism; he also retains, in a non-handicraft sense, the virtues of craft.

The craft ingredient in contemporary mainstream domestic design is potent. In Britain one
9–12 company that specializes in good design and offers an echo of almost Shakeresque workmanship is Miles/Carter Limited, where the designer, Ronald Carter, has produced a range of domestic pieces of great quality. His dining chairs, for example, tend to be ample in their proportions without ever being too heavy or uncomfortable to lift. Similarly, a chest of drawers or a cupboard genuinely function as storage units, as well as visually satisfying pieces of design. Always the work, made in a factory in the north of England, is well produced.

In the same light it is interesting that Ettore Sottsass, having emerged from Memphis, has recently shed the carapace of avant-garde radicalism and designed one of his most beautiful and serviceable pieces of furniture — a chair which, unusually for him, plays up its craft element. The chair is called Bridge and it is manufactured by Knoll International. The design owes some of its thinking to Danish furniture, but more specifically it owes its structure to Chinese designs of the 17th century. The construction round the base of the seat is a particularly strong characteristic of Chinese work.

33   Bridge raises, again, the matter of historical quotation and reference. Design, like art, is a communal activity. Designers do not work in isolation from either their peers or history. Nostalgia may stink, but it would be foolish not to use the compositional recipes that have been discovered. What matters is that the contemporary designer should remain in control of his design. To use established design recipes as a fundamental part of one's own design thinking is different from simply seizing on likely quotations in order to make up for a lack of thought.

The craft element introduced by Sottsass contributes to the chair's domesticated look. It looks a most comfortable object. The popular idea of the home is predicated on an ideal of comfort, but comfort as a reality has at least two elements to it. There is physical comfort – and this is dependent upon a design that understands how the furniture will feel on the bodies of those using it; and there is wellbeing. Wellbeing is not wholly related to ample upholstery and soft cushions. It includes the textures that feed the touch and the eye. Moreover, there is the user's sense of dignity, his or her psychological comfort.

Consider, for example, the 1960s debut of the Sacco armchair by Paolini, Gatti and Teodoro (Italy). Saccos were large leather sacks (cheaper versions were made from canvas) stuffed with tiny polystyrene balls. They may have owed something of their design pedigree to the soft sculptures of Claes Oldenburg, the American pop art sculptor. Saccos were sloppy and alleged to be comfortable. The theory appeared straightforward – a Sacco took on the shape of the person who sank into it. The spirit was very much of the late 1960s, when everyone was supposed to level down – which, in a Sacco, was inevitable. Eventually, it was admitted that the Sacco was physically uncomfortable and most people felt ill at ease looking and feeling as though they were stranded in a large and wilful doughnut. Sacco, the metaphor for laissez-faire democracy, was defeated by its inability to encourage wellbeing.

Metaphor in design can obviously strengthen or undermine wellbeing. The Italian company, Poltrona Frau, expert in the use of leather, has sustained a design look that is essentially rooted in the clubbable atmosphere of the 1920s ocean-going liners, although in truth the design pedigrees of chairs such as 1919 and Vanity Fair (simple, leather armchairs) go back to 19th-century England. Poltrona Frau has commissioned designers such as Mario Zanuso, Pierluigi Cerri and F. A. Porsche for contemporary work, but the Poltrona Frau clientele is rich, conservative and status conscious.

The Italians, who have the undoubted edge in radical domestic design, retain that edge in all design, including quasi-traditional styling. Consider the Club chair by Alessandro Mendini – it 26 works, it is a classic, and it is a patriarchal chair, an appropriate metaphor for the Italian domestic scene in which the family head is a man even if popular sentiment reveres mama.

More recent, innovative designs, very good in their way, are more divisive in whom they appeal to – their metaphorical content is not conciliatory. Take, for example, the modern recliner, which has become a classic 20th-century domestic artefact – for designers. Recliners, like beds, are only appropriate where you feel secure; you do not stretch out where you feel vulnerable. Only drunks, secure in their oblivion, stretch out on park benches, for example.

The advantage of the modern recliner over the ordinary sofa is that sofas do not normally possess variable geometry and certainly have nothing to compare with the following examples: the Porsche 84 S, and the variable recliner by Jan Lade and Svein Asbjørnsen. 49–51

Dining chair. Anonymous.   Chromed steel, red vinyl.
USA, c. 1955

Chaise Longue. Richard Schultz for Knoll International. Aluminium, vinyl and Dacron webbing. USA, 1966

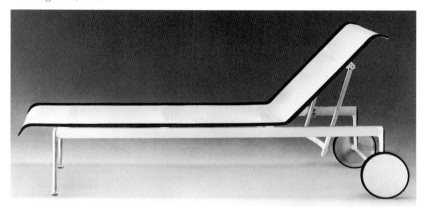

The Porsche 84 S was designed for the West German manufacturer InterProfil by F. A. Porsche, who also designed the famous Porsche 904 and 911 sports cars. It is an impressive object, visually loud, and its styling is rather aggressive. This is a seat that is unrelentingly masculine and exclusive: it radiates quality, engineering and money. The 84 S is a serious object on which to recline: one's topics of conversation will be robust rather than flighty.

The imagery of the 84 S is taken from the idea of a machine. Porsche publicity asserts: 'The functional objective alone has given rise to the structure and form of this chair.' You sit upright and push down, and wherever you stop pushing, that is the angle at which you recline – there is a torsion steel spring system that holds the back and the seat (both move) in place. The seat and the back operate via a sliding mechanism and for reasons too complicated to explain you need to acquire a knack of flexing your calf muscles in order to come up from being down.

The 84 S raises the question as to whether or not the metaphor of the machine is an appropriate one for the living room. When Poltrona Frau commissioned F. A. Porsche to design a recliner, they commissioned a design that was altogether more gentle. Called the Antropovarius, it is an anthropomorphic-looking chaise longue which is constructed on a disc-and-bone principle that is analogous to the structure of the human spine. It was thoroughly researched and designed so that the back rest can be inclined, the foot rest lengthened and the armchair split into three sections by two main joints. However, the logic and engineering is disguised in rich, very soft leather.

The electrically operated recliner by the Norwegian designers Jan Lade and Svein Asbjørnsen may go too far for some tastes in its attempt to rationalize comfort. Lade and Asbjørnsen have made various designs for comfortable, stretch-yourself-out seating and their Stressless Spirit, a chair with a foot stool, is comfortable and domestically respectable. But their electric recliner, apart from looking so obviously like an electric engine, also shouts 'orthopaedics' at you. The recliner is sensible and socially responsible design for the elderly or infirm because all one need do is press a button to change position. But metaphorically such a reminder of infirmity in the living room is tactless, like placing a surgical boot on the dining table.

The belief that comfort is a natural consequence of good posture has resulted in a lively market for scientifically researched furniture. The Westnofa company of Norway is famous for its sound posture furniture and its Balans range, developed initially by Peter Opsvik, is sold all 22 over the world. One of the more recent Balans pieces is the Gravity chair, which can be rocked into one of four stable positions. It goes from desk or table position to full back, and no doubt has its place in the range of domestic body language as you flip through the stages of rapt vertical attention to sharp, horizontal dismissal.

Many people find the Balans range comfortable. Moreover, designers such as Opsvik and Svein Gusrud, one of Opsvik's contemporaries, are showing a commitment to the idea of service to the consumer. Naturally there is some shrewd marketing here as well; by inventing furniture which displays its ergonomic intentions so blatantly, the furniture market has been widened. It is better to widen a market than seek to compete in it on the same lines as everyone else.

The most famous Balans design is the successful Balans Kneeler, now in several versions. No doubt this piece has its own design pedigree, but it is interesting how so few ideas are entirely original. For example, the Primate chair of Achille Castiglioni (Italy) dates from 1970 and looks 6 rather similar to the Balans (the critical difference is in the variation allowed to the body – you can either rock the Balans forward or back, or, in some versions, adjust the angle of the seat). Although Castiglioni's Primate has an ergonomic theme and resulted from 'an urge to strip the chair back to its ergonomic essentials', Ospvik's chair had the benefit of more recent research.

Of course, potential criticism of the good posture design movement again centres on the notion of wellbeing. The Scandinavians in general and the Norwegians in particular do not seem to mind putting themselves in eccentric positions – perhaps this self-confidence stems from the fact that physically they tend to be good looking and robust, and place a high premium on health; but for the physically less homogeneously good looking and less athletic urban masses of Britain or the United States the physical-fitness furniture is not so attractive. Something similar applies to high couture fashion: the short, the gangling, the fat and the ugly find themselves made to look more ridiculous than is fair.

However, the Scandinavians have kept alive in design an understanding of the importance of variety in surfaces and the contribution to wellbeing of natural textures. Leading designers from other countries are also proclaiming the importance of natural materials. In September 1986 the magazine *domus* made much of Ettore Sottsass's comment: 'Objects are beautiful when there are at least two materials; two poles which produce electricity.' The article, which is in praise of Sottsass's Bridge and Mandarin chairs, then continues: 'In these chairs electricity runs smoothly through materials which are natural, sweet and simple like wood, sand, very old cloth and pieces of pottery.'

33, 34

In fact the expressive qualities obtained through contrasting materials or contrasting forms or colours is one of the oldest (and most useful) strategies available to the designer, architect, artist, gardener or cook. The emotional and expressive qualities of old textures (with all their associative qualities of time and mortality) have long been realized and cherished by craftsmen-designers (see Chapter 4). Indeed, one of the virtues of the 20th-century craft movement has been to keep alive the variety of visual and tactile texture that designers, especially those of the modern movement, overlooked or derided. It is, however, of interest that Sottsass should be arguing for a return to natural textures (as does Branzi), and so have caught up with the craftsmen and applied artists.

In general there has been a loss of expressive surfaces in the average contemporary home. The widespread use of dull plastic veneers trying to pretend they are wood, or polyurethane varnishes that bounce the light hard back at you in an unremitting stare, has not been an aesthetic gain (although such surfaces are easy to clean). Against such a dispiriting background the temporary championing by Sottsass and Branzi of plastic laminates with new and lively abstract patterns took on some significance and attracted interest within the design community. However, artificial wood cladding, the now traditional role of plastic veneer, is always disappointing because it never looks like the real thing.

The causes of this disappointment are as much factual as psychological: an artificial cladding will probably be too symmetrical in its colouring or even in the distribution of its 'accidental' patterning; it will not reflect (or absorb) light the way natural wood does. Eventually, we can construct the explanation of why the false wood cladding is ultimately bound to fail.

There is no avoiding the basic principle adhered to by the modern movement designers and the best of 20th-century craftsmen alike – truth to materials. And the vanguard of design for the domestic landscape is, happily, shared by designers whose instincts are both respectful of materials and whose touch is generally light, easy and full of grace. Many of these designers are well known: they include Shiro Kuramata (Japan) and Enzo Mari (Italy).

1, 40
63

Kuramata's work is an elegant demonstration of design synthesis: synthesis between modern movement directness of form and a decorative sense that can only be described as 'flair' – it is the sense that some people have of rightness, the way they throw a cover over a chair, or wear a shawl, or arrange objects on a table. Kuramata is also master of the much commented upon gift that seems to be an innate part of Japanese culture: an ability to handle pattern. This shows itself in design not simply as surface decoration but in the graceful repetition of such elements as handles, knobs and drawers. His art lies in the ease with which his materials do his work. There is no stress in Kuramata's imagery – hence they present themselves gently.

Enzo Mari has set a standard that has become one of the benchmarks of contemporary design thinking. Mari is an intellectual who believes that once a piece of furniture design has been solved there is no point in dabbling with it further (compare Erik de Graaff's comments about furniture design in Chapter 4). Mari's Sof Sof chair, first brought into manufacture by Driade in 1972, remains one of the masterpieces of contemporary design. The structure is made up from nine grey lacquered tubular iron rings that are welded together; the seat and back are two cushions of grey leather. His Delfina chair is a kind of gossamer-thin concoction: it is a lovely aerial thing that makes a mockery – both as functional and as decorative object – of the pretentiousness of the overweight ornamentalist styles. His tables are very simple: they are like grammatical sentences in plain words. You can deduce the thinking that conceived them from their construction. The technology they depend upon is unsophisticated. All Mari's work is as easily suited for mass production as for small backstreet workshops. His work makes you look with a fresh eye at the work of others.

In my view Mari anticipated the late-1980s trend (confirmed by Ettore Sottsass, Philippe Starck and Alessandro Mendini) for synthesis – a domestic middle way between the extreme celebration of the new world which the modern movement provided and the frantic nostalgia which post-modernism encouraged. The middle way is always the right away for homes.

76

Opposite
1 Apple Honey
  Shiro Kuramata
  Anodized metal
  h. 75 cm
  Japan, 1985

2 Finger chair
  Gijs Bakker
  Bent plywood
  h. 75 cm
  Holland, 1979

3 Strip chair
  Gijs Bakker for Castelijn
  Bentwood
  h. 75 cm
  Holland, 1974

4 Torsion chair (prototype)
  Gijs Bakker
  Bentwood
  h. 65 cm
  Holland, 1973–77

5 Folding chair
Gijs Bakker
Painted wood
h. 75 cm
Holland, 1976

6 Oikos-due
  Antonia Astori for Driade
  Pressed wood with melamine covering
  Max.h. 2.7 m
  Italy, 1980

7 Prototype kitchen (homage to McDonalds)
  Antonia Astoria for Driade
  Pressed wood with melamine covering
  h. 2.7 m
  Italy, 1982

8 Kitchen system
  Antonia Astoria for Driade
  Pressed wood with melamine covering
  Max.h. 2.7 m
  Italy, 1982

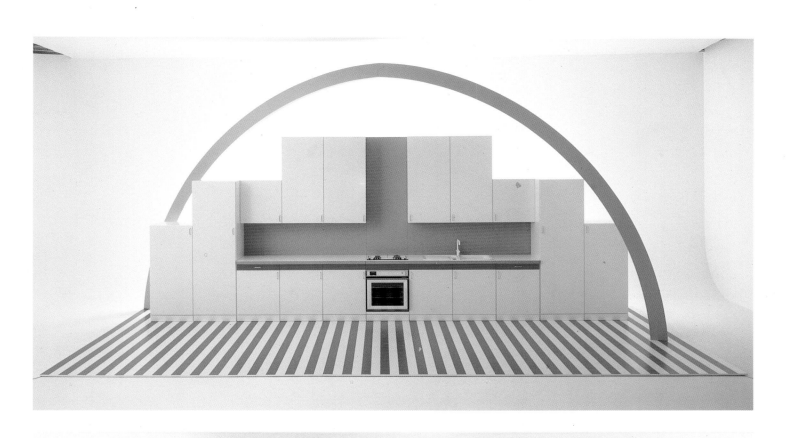

9 Witney tallboy
Ronald Carter for Miles/Carter
Oak
h. 1.8 m
UK, 1982

10 Bloomsbury side table
Ronald Carter for Miles/Carter
Oak
h. 71 cm
UK, 1985

11 Haarlem chair
Ronald Carter for Miles/Carter
Timber frame, foam, webbing seat, wool cover
h. 92 cm
UK, 1983

12 Witney fixed top table
Ronald Carter for Miles/Carter
Oak
h. 72 cm
UK, 1981

13 Von Vogelsang
    Philippe Starck for Driade
    Bent and perforated iron
    h. 71 cm
    France, 1984

14 Tippy Jackson folding table
    Philippe Starck for Driade
    Varnished iron
    h. 71 cm
    France, 1982

15 Titos Apostos folding table
    Philippe Starck for Driade
    Iron
    d. 85 cm
    France, 1985

16 Door handle (detail)
    Jasper Morrison
    Chromed, sandblasted steel
    l. 15 cm
    UK, 1986

17 Bedroom cupboards
    Jasper Morrison
    Medium-density fibreboard
    h. 2.4 m
    UK, 1986

18 Stressless Spirit
    Svein Asbjørnsen and Jan Lade
    Steel, wood, upholstery
    h. 106 cm
    Norway, 1985

19,20 Pratfall
  21 Philippe Starck
     Bent plywood back, iron tube
     h. 86 cm
     France, 1982

  22 Balans variable seating
     Peter Opsvik for Westnofa
     Steel, upholstery
     h. 90 cm
     Norway, 1985

23 Prima
   Mario Botta
   Steel, epoxy painted
   h. 75 cm
   Italy, 1982

24 Chairs
   Pentti Hakala
   Chromed steel, bentwood
   h. 75 cm
   Finland, 1986

25 Sofa
Robert Venturi for Knoll International
Wood, upholstery
l. 2.1 m
USA, 1984

26 San Leonardo Collection
Alessandro Mendini
Leather, wood frame
h. 1 m
Italy, 1985

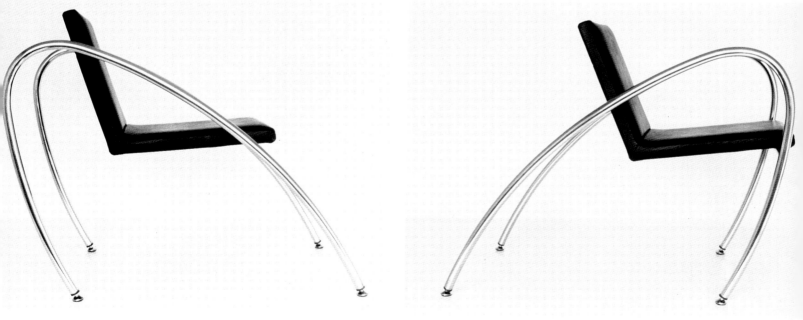

27 Mezzo chair and
   pivoting table
   Flux Design (Paul
      Chamberlain and Peter
      Christian) for Hoskins
   Steel
   h. 60 cm
   UK, 1985–86

28,29 Nemo Edition
   Alain Domingo and
      Françoise Scali
   Chromed steel, leather
   h. 76 cm
   Italy, 1984

30 Table
   Mathew Hilton for
      Sheridan Coakley
   Tubular steel
   h. 90 cm
   UK, 1985

31 Trolley
   Mathew Hilton for
      Sheridan Coakley
   Tubular steel, glass
   h. 83 cm
   UK, 1986

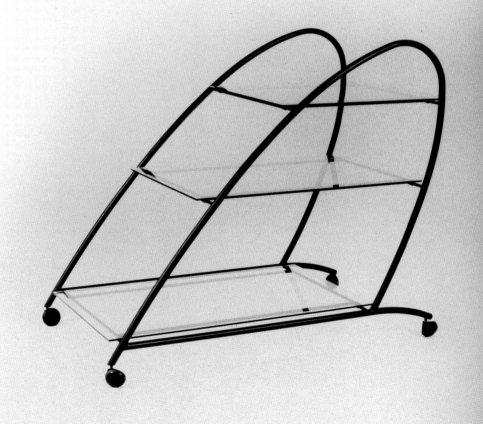

32 Tokyo chairs and stool
   Rodney Kinsman for OMK
   Steel tube, polyurethane foam back
   h. 70 cm, 90 cm
   UK, 1985

33 Bridge
   Ettore Sottsass for Knoll International
   Tubular steel, polyurethane foam
   h. 75 cm
   Italy, 1986

34 Mandarin
   Ettore Sottsass for Knoll International
   Beech
   h. 75 cm
   Italy, 1986

35,36 4873 chair
37,38 Anna Castelli Ferrieri for Kartell
       Polypropylene
       h. 75 cm
       Italy, 1985

41 Veranda
    Vico Magistretti for Cassina
    Steel folding frame, polyurethane foam,
      fabric or leather, steel base
    h. 1.1 m
    Italy, 1983

42 Veranda 3
   Vico Magistretti for Cassina
   Wooden base, polyurethane
      foam, fabric or leather
   h. 1.1 m
   Italy, 1984

43 Villabianca 1
   Vico Magistretti for Cassina
   Beechwood, polyester seat shell,
      fabric or leather
   h. 78 cm
   Italy, 1985

44 Edison
   Vico Magistretti for Cassina
   Birch or glass top, steel base
   h. 72 cm
   Italy, 1985

45 Cardigan
   Vico Magistretti for Cassina
   Wood frame, leather or fabric
   h. 1.05 m
   Italy, 1986

46 Queen Anne chair
Robert Venturi for Knoll International
Bent plywood
h. 88 cm
USA, 1984

47 Sheraton, left; Art Deco, right
Robert Venturi for Knoll International
Plywood with silkscreen appliqué
h. 75 cm
USA, 1984

48 The Venturi Collection
Robert Venturi for Knoll International
USA, 1984

49 Split Returner
Svein Asbjørnsen and Jan Lade
Steel, upholstery, electric motor
l. 2 m
Norway, 1986

50,51 84 S Recliner
F. A. Porsche for InterProfil
Steel, leather
l. 1.50 m
West Germany, 1984

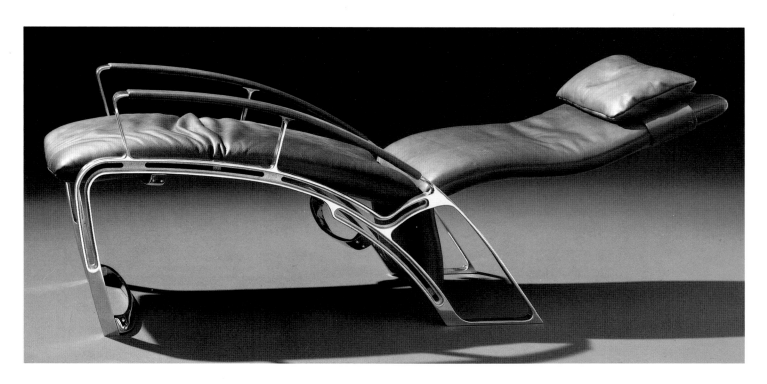

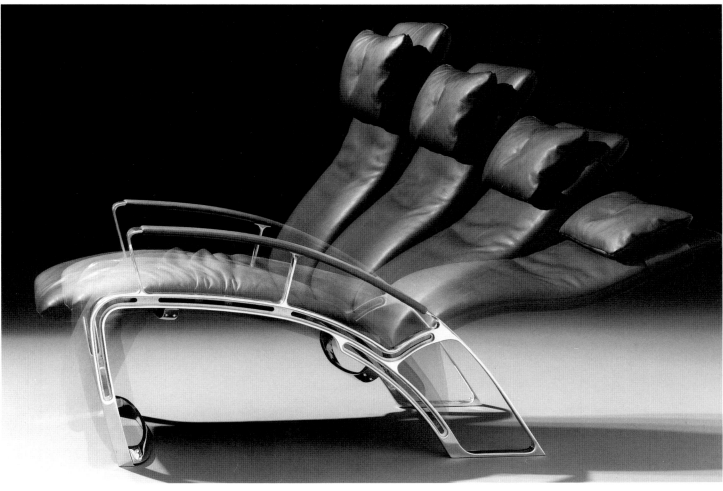

52 Totem
   Torstein Nilsen
   Wood
   h. 90 cm
   Norway, 1985

53,54 Bibi'Bibo
   Massimo Morozzi for Driade
   Lacquered wood
   l. 2.08 m
   Italy, 1983

55 Capitello
Enzo Mari for Driade
Wood
h. 72 cm
Italy, 1977

56 Teatro
Aldo Rossi and Luca Meda
Lacquered wood
h. 75 cm
Italy, 1982

57 Chair
Philippe Starck
Tubular steel
h. 75 cm
France, 1985

58 Chaise longue from the
King's Furniture collection
Rud Thygesen and Johnny Sørensen
O'ak, plaited cane
l. 1.40 m
Denmark, 1984

59 Desk, armchair
Rud Thygesen and Johnny Sørensen
Beech
h. 73 cm (desk)
Denmark, 1971

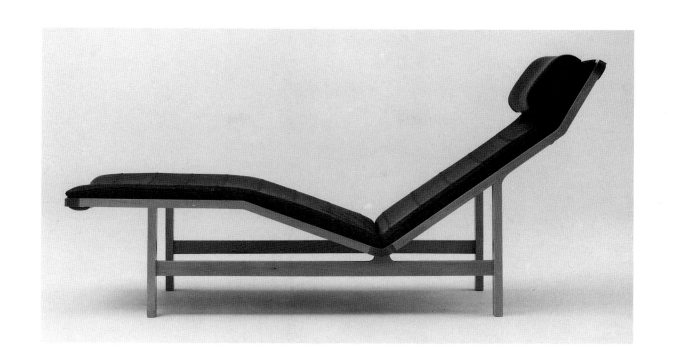

60 Chair
    George Sowden
    Painted wood
    h. 90 cm
    Italy/UK, 1986

61,62 Armchair
       George Sowden
       Painted wood
       h. 90 cm
       Italy/UK, 1986

63 How high the moon
    Shiro Kuramata
    Steel
    h. 80 cm
    Japan, 1986

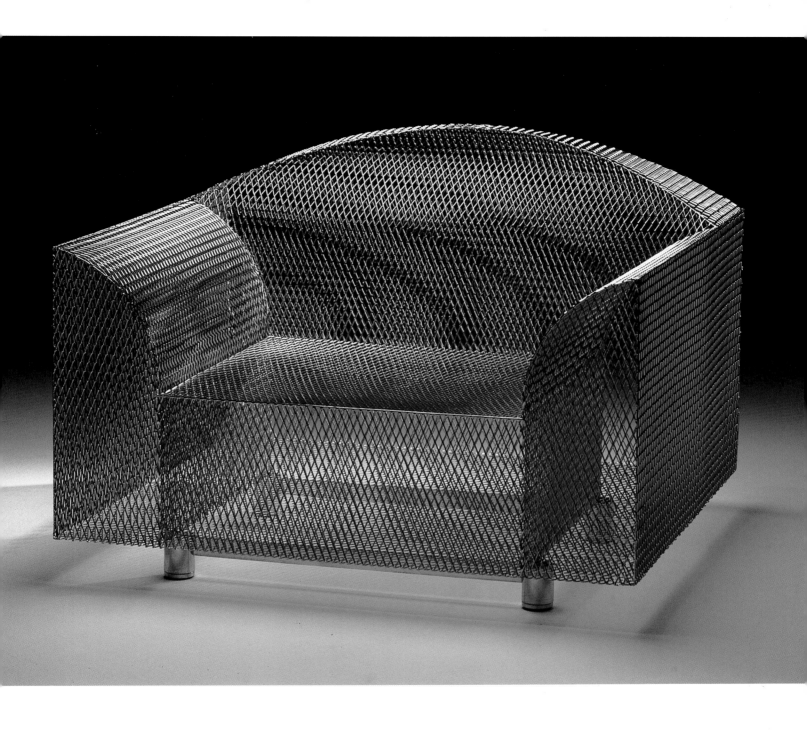

64 Café
   Pelikan Designs for Fritz Hansen
   Steel tube, grey rubber seat
   h. 60 cm
   Denmark, 1983

65 Stool
   Alan Peters
   Ash
   h. 30 cm
   UK, 1976

66 Primate
   Achille Castiglioni for Zanotta
   Steel, vinyl-upholstered
   h. 47 cm
   Italy, 1970

67 Balans duo
   Peter Opsvik
   Wood
   h. 45 cm
   Norway, 1980

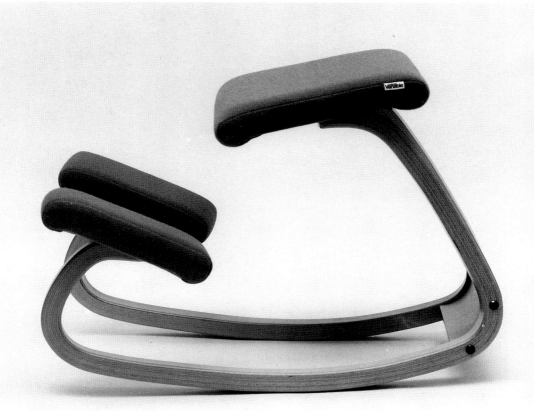

'69'89 70,71
Outdoor chaise longue,
    prototype
Gijs Bakker
Aluminium, fabric
l. 1.6 m
Holland, 1980

72 Console
    Anna Anselmi for Bieffeplast
    Steel frame, regenerated marble
    h. 73 cm
    Italy, 1985

73,74 Chair, bench, armchair
   75 Anna Anselmi for Bieffeplast
       Steel frame, epoxy finished
       h. 85 cm
       Italy, 1985

76 Sof Sof
    Enzo Mari for Driade
    Nine grey iron rings, leather
    h. 84 cm
    Italy, 1971

77 Addenda modular storage and work system
    Tony Wills for the Futon Company
    Medium-density fibreboard
    h. 1.8 m
    UK, 1986

78 Grey triangles
    Rei Kawakubo for Pallucco
    Iron tube and granite
    h. 73 cm
    Japan/Italy, 1986

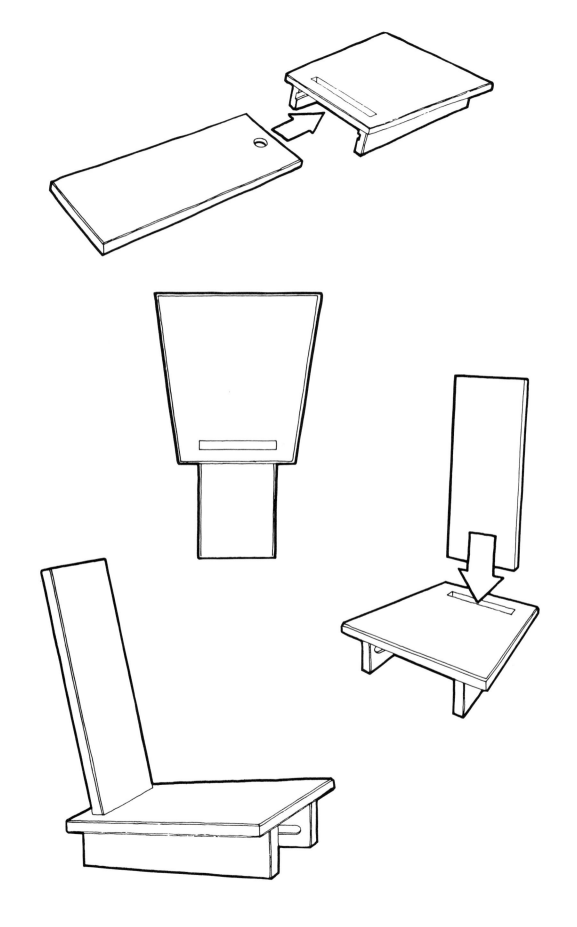

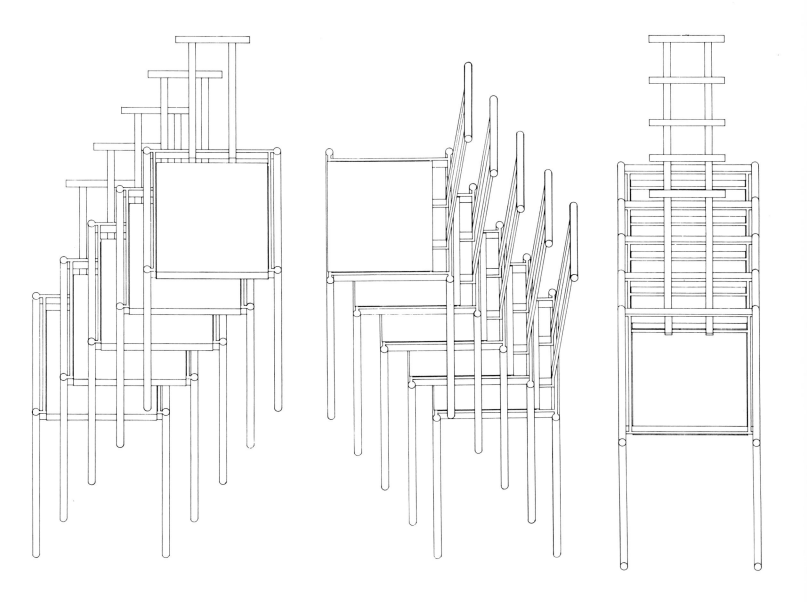

79 Futon chair, drawings
    Tony Wills
    Oak, medium-density fibreboard
    h. 30 cm
    UK, 1985

80 Elle stacking chair, drawings
    Eleanor Wood
    Tubular, strip and perforated steel
    Chair stacks within 26 mm
    h. 75 cm
    UK, 1985

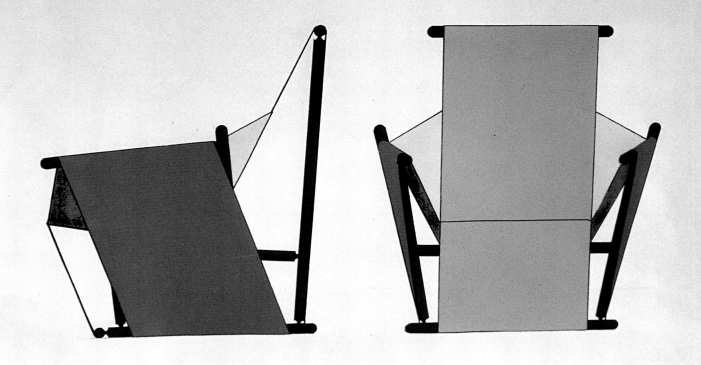

DESIGN FOR AN EASY CHAIR MOTTO 'KIMONO' IN CANVAS AND DOWELLING
© JAAK FLORIS VAN DEN BROECKE mdesrca JULY 1983 DRWG & DEV ANNELIES DE LEEDE

81 Canvas chair, drawing
   Floris van den Broecke
   Canvas, wood
   h. 80 cm
   Holland/UK, 1983

3

LIVING WITH THE SYSTEM

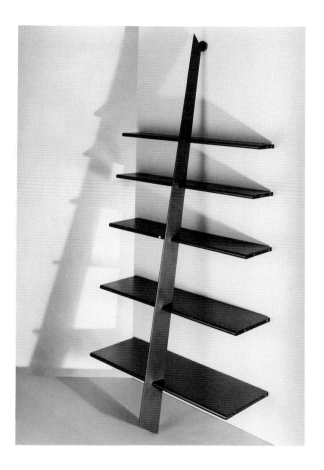

Mac Gee shelving unit. Philippe Starck. France, 1984

Design for the contract market

Furnishing the modern office provides several design challenges. For example, the office furniture manufacturer is generally hoping for big orders; what he sells must not be too idiosyncratic in its visual personality. And, although no office is the same as another, few companies want to commission tailor-made designs. Consequently, the contract furniture manufacturer must ape the car manufacturer and provide serviceable ranges that will adequately fulfil the demands of different individuals.

Cost constraints are formidable because the office market is competitive (although not as severely so as the domestic market). Nevertheless, many designers have done their best work for the office. Design-led furniture manufacturers such as Castelli (Italy) and Sunar Hauserman (USA) prefer the contract office to the domestic market where good design can be compromised more easily by razor-thin profit margins and conservative taste. The office manager, perhaps surprisingly, tolerates a measure of design innovation, as well as being attentive to technological development.

The office offers challenges to the designer in four quarters: aesthetics, technology, architecture and social engineering.

Aesthetics: Most companies have a very clear idea of the kind of image they want to project. The creation of appropriate metaphor in office design is one of the designer's key tasks. Here you can see different interpretations of what this means: the Morrison system (USA) is visually very quiet, a blank slate on which a corporation makes its mark, whereas Richard Sapper's system for Castelli is strong and sculptured — it is emphatically modern.

86–88

Technology: Apart from the rapid and rampant developments in information technology, which have affected the design of desks and work stations (with Tecno's Nomos system offering the most intriguing and perhaps flexible wire management service), some aspects of office chair design have become major feats of mechanical and materials engineering — see, for example, Mario Bellini's Figura and Persona chairs.

99
111–113
119, 120

Architecture: the integration of architecture and design has become an aesthetic ambition of the late 1980s. The major office design houses present their works in an appropriate architectural setting. For example, Sunar Hauserman called in the architect Michael Graves to design furniture and provide an appropriate setting for his own work and the other ranges

82

marketed by the company. However, in terms of the architecture created by office systems, the extremes are Tecno's Nomos system – no partitions at all – and Herman Miller's Ethospace system, which uses the office wall and partition technique imaginatively and solidly to create architecture within a building.

Social engineering: Managers and designers alike recognize that office work can be tedious. The tedium is made worse for many people (mostly women) by new technology; thus a sociology of office design is developing to mix efficiency with humanity. Possibly Ethospace is the system most centred on social behaviour, but no good designer now ignores the importance of serving employees with intelligent and reassuring work spaces. The most individual answer to the problem of suiting individual taste is Vincenzo Iavicoli and Maria Luisa Rossi's Walking Office (Italy).

127–131

OFFICE SYSTEMS

The three most important features of an office are having interesting work, a window and defensible space. Defensible space has intrigued design theorists for some years and the biggest development in response to its challenges was the introduction of the 'systems' concept. In the mid-1960s West German design theorists evolved the concept of *Bürlandschaft* design, which meant 'office landscape' – it entailed flexibility, units of furniture that could be arranged and rearranged in configurations across the open office floor. The open office was the great (and to some eyes, now dubious) invention that accompanied the office-block building which started in the 19th century. In the 1960s it began to be thought that it might be kinder to have the space broken up by low walls and so to break away from the 19th-century schoolroom model, with its manager overseer in a glass-walled box at the far end.

The logic of the *Bürolandschaft* approach would work only with a system of furniture units that would be of standard dimensions, with a limited range of fittings. The systems idea introduced a new vocabulary – 'work station', 'desking' and 'module'. A number of manufacturers quickly picked up the challenge: the notion of mass production of a limited number of parts designed to form a greater number of configurations for any space had great economic appeal. Among the earliest in the field was the English company Hille, which in 1963 had already anticipated systems design with their Hille Storage Wall System; but the company which set the standard for office systems furniture was Herman Miller (USA) which, in 1968, launched Action Office. Action Office was the first fully flexible, integrated-module orientated system. It was an enormous success and is still in production, albeit in an updated version: the company is happy and loud in its proclamation that the system has achieved sales of $2.5 billion so far.

Left, Desk. Gerard Taylor. Steel frame, work surface covered in panels of leather, briar veneer, grey paint. UK, 1984

Right, Morrison office system (Executive version). Andrew Morrison for Knoll International. USA, 1986

Office furniture and its design is bound in with (or ought to be bound in with) the work and management policy of the office. Occasionally one is granted a view of the adult 'office' that is playful. Consider the trading floor of a major financial trading house in New York, London or Tokyo. Essentially the modern trading floor is a large quasi-theatrical space (trade is a kind of drama) where hundreds of dealers get frantic in front of one another. The dealers' desks are tightly packed together because the dealers need to yell information at one another. They seem to like the excitement caused by the critical mass – it is still largely a male world, like one of those ball games in which men delight in falling together in a heap.

The controlled anarchy and the enthusiastic competitiveness of the dealers is obviously not a common model of management for most offices. At most offices a good system is generally regarded as one which affords management a high degree of control, as well as a pleasanter environment. However, apart from creating a network of defensible spaces and breaking up the serried rank monotony of the open office, the earlier office systems – or rather their layouts – tended to degenerate into a mess of mazes. Some offices got lost in the potted plants and during the 1970s it gradually emerged that what was wanted was an office which balanced order and formality with friendliness, but not with disorder. People were also complaining of high noise levels.

Acknowledging that the systems idea was ripe for further development, Herman Miller evolved Ethospace, launched in 1986. The core of the Ethospace concept is flexibility. It is a   92–96

wide-ranging system extending from typists' work stations to executives' suites, and includes meeting rooms and conference areas. Meeting space is important. The fast increase in information technology is resulting in information of all kinds, and people seem to prefer to talk face-to-face and not through their computers.

The designer of Ethospace, Bill Stumpf, did not want his design to look overtly like a system because systems are, in his view, emotionally offensive to many people. No one wants to feel like a cipher. The give-away with systems' walls and work surfaces is the seam. Stumpf added many more seams to create walls that allude to the construction of brick or stone and in fact echo the proportions of Japanese houses. Stumpf also rejected over-playing the tactic of hanging shelves and cabinets off walls: each time a shelf or horizontal plane is wanted a vertical wall is needed, which in turn results in too many walls — too many walls make a maze.

Lighting, especially natural light, is prized by Stumpf. Windows frame views and give you contact with the outside world. And in dumping the office-as-machine metaphor, Stumpf has highlighted two intriguing aspects of the nature of office work.

First, Stumpf argues: 'Somehow, office work has become almost pornographic.' He thinks that there is a social barrier in offices to bouts of hard concentration behind a closed door and remarks: 'the big no-no in the modern office is any form of social withdrawal'. The result is that people either come in very early, stay very late, or do their concentrated work at home. Serious work, he concludes, often occurs in unconventional places and at unconventional times.

The second aspect is Stumpf's concept of 'gratuitous difficulty'. The design orthodoxy is that everything should be to hand, but clearly, if one wants a break, then it is helpful if things are not to hand. You may want to walk to the window to use the telephone, reasons Stumpf, or have a change of space for reading or writing.

There is an irritating hearthside bonhomie to Ethospace's marketing, caused partly by the homely anecdotes that feature Bill Stumpf's grandfather. However, the point of the 'play' or added interest component in humdrum activities is important and well made by Stumpf as he recalls: 'My grandfather from Switzerland was enormously attached to his toys. His whole day was a matter of gratuitous difficulty. Most of us put the shaving cream on, whip a blade over our faces, take a stand-up shower. He had a night cap, a gown and socks which he wore to bed in his freezing cold room. He'd get up, boil water, pour it in this big porcelain bowl, put a fresh towel in there – so hot you could barely touch it – put in on his face and walk around the kitchen singing to his canaries . . . He had cuckoo clocks and cigar clippers and a million little things to do every day . . . He lived to be almost 100.'

Yet women may wonder how much work such men as Stumpf's very agreeable-sounding grandfather actually generate for wives or daughters or secretaries, and accountants will naturally cry out that a clerk is a clerk is a clerk and he (but usually she) is not employed to wind up cuckoo clocks. Moreover, a critical design factor in New York, Tokyo and Europe will be the cost per square foot of the space used; play space is profit space. Nevertheless, if, as Stumpf is arguing, variety can be introduced into the working area, then efficiency will increase because people will be happier. Unhappy people are subversive and rotten workers. Howard Brenton's and David Hare's fictional South African newspaper magnate, Lambert Le Roux, remarks in their play *Pravda* (London, 1986): 'I keep on trying to push the little people into holes. But they won't stay in. They wriggle, they keep popping out. They refuse to be happy in there.'

The concept of gratuitous difficulty echoes Robert Venturi's thoughts on contradiction and complexity, and parallels a belief of Andrea Branzi's that all the objects we design and place should take their cue from the way the individual wants to live and act. Stumpf, Venturi and Branzi have each argued the one post-modern principle that designers would be foolish to ignore: people get bored with simple tasks and plain views. People want complexity in what they see and in what they do; continuous distraction appears to be a fundamental human need. Such a point may not be profound, but it has tended to be ignored because it has been assumed that individual ways of doing things cannot be plotted into ergonomic and rationalist plans that are intended to work for the majority. Herman Miller argue that with the right 'loose-fit' system, you can afford to be individual.

Ethospace looks good. The inclusion of quality wood surfaces that run down to the edges like a seashore ensure that the actual feel and the perceived feel are soft but not sloppy. The design of the walls, with their windows and gentle colours and the fine detailing where each segment abuts, is successful – moreover, it looks architectural. The 'architectural' quality is important now that in the late 1980s the concept of 'space planning' has again become more an aesthetic activity, as well as a pseudo-scientific or economic one. The architectural element in systems office furniture has psychological value because it suggests a degree of permanence. Defensible individual spaces or domesticated conference spaces can be undermined by the suggestion that the place has been slapped up with temporary infills.

The role of metaphor in the Ethospace system is subtle: the imagery aimed at is a generalized one of quality and wellbeing – modernism without the frigidness of work-study neurosis. The role of metaphor in office furniture is seldom overt: you do not usually find literary or narrative images there; when a company wants to 'make a statement' it usually commissions a series of one-off designs for the Chairman's office.

135   Thus Knoll International's (USA) recent strategy is interesting. Knoll launched the Morrison system in 1986. It is aurally deadening because its panels are designed to provide sound insulation. Morrison is extensive and can be made to serve either an individual work station or a conference room. Like all serious modern office systems Morrison takes care of storage, lighting and wire management efficiently. Morrison is certainly a tidy system, but some critics say it is dull, the design equivalent of the silent housewife niggard. Knoll argues that a system which is visually 'quiet', which does not impose itself on the eye, is the visual corollary of hiding away its services – it is intended to function without fuss, without you realizing it is there. The underlying metaphor speaks of the 'corporation' – polite but disclosing only the face that is deemed circumspect: just like the side of a skyscraper built in the International Style.

Like Herman Miller, Knoll International has a history of casting wide its net for designers. Among the younger Europeans to interest Knoll is Paul Atkinson (UK), who in 1985 submitted to Knoll a proposal for a new desking system.

97, 98   Atkinson's work gives an insight into the way good design achieves a balance between metaphor, construction and function. Atkinson chose to design a frame-based desk system because he wanted a language of space, light and shade – not mass. He wanted an analogy with modern architecture and adopted the I-beam for both metaphorical and practical purposes. Metaphorical because the I-beam is the modern building component for bridging and spanning spaces – it is the symbol of the New York skyscraper. It is also good at providing rigidity and strength: its weight-to-strength ratio is good, which in turn means that its strength-to-cost ratio is good.

The architectural I-beam is made from rolled steel, and the rolling of hot metal does not provide the right texture and finish for furniture. So Atkinson went for extruded aluminium instead. This decision gave him further lightness: it allowed him to have a hollow core, which in turn enabled him to develop the connecting nodes that marry into the I-beams. The connecting nodes have holes in them – into which pellets of glue are inserted – and when the node is slid into the frame and the unit heated to melt the glue, the bonding is very strong and sealed for life. This removes the need for bolts. Apart from the aesthetic improvement resulting from getting away from a structure that looks like a warship, there is a technical gain, for the bonding is stronger than conventional bolts. The angles of the connecting nodes allow two important developments – at the bottom, where they may connect to castors or sliders, they act like outriggers or stabilizers giving more stability to the desk; at the top, where any kind of surface can be supported by the nodes, the plane of the desk top is lifted up and away from the frame, allowing for all the wiring for telephones and computer terminals to be housed in trays.

Aesthetics are vital. In order to give the I-beams definition, Atkinson added a beading to each – it not only looks better, it feels better: your fingers run up and down tracing the parallel lines. In the end, the literal references to I-beams and the skyscraper are irrelevant to the client because he or she is concerned only with the composition as it is presented – the metaphorical logic is of more importance to the designer in that it gives him a method for organizing his forms. Process is of importance only to the practitioner, not the user.

One of the most significant new designs in office furniture is Norman Foster's (UK) Nomos range, commissioned by the Italian company Tecno. Nomos demonstrates that the intellectual momentum of the modern movement has strength to outface the quirkiness of post-modern reaction. Foster is one of the world's leading architects. He is an untypical Englishman: he believes in progress, in technology and in modern possibilities. Each of his buildings is an optimistic exploration of light and the excitement of precise positioning of planes in three dimensions. He has put this excitement in his office furniture.

Tecno's brief was as follows: the desk must cope with more than one terminal (the wire management issue was central); the system had to be flexible, so that the office layout could be easily altered; the desk had to be capable of adaptation by the user (in fact, it can be used as a desk, table, drawing board or even lectern). As a result, the large thin black-laminate work surfaces are placed apparently in mid-air, fully adjustable as drawing boards. From one work station to another, like the backbone of a sea serpent, there is a black clip on-spine which carries the wires of lights, telephones, computer terminals and so forth. The wires are laced in. Storage for papers, drawing, print-outs is above the work space, but at the point of writing further storage is being designed. Stone- and glasswork surfaces can be used, and the supporting structures resemble the legs of lunar landing vehicles. Foster's design demonstrates complexity and contradiction without once renouncing the promise of progress, or the possibilities of the present.

Nomos is beautiful. The workmanship and detailing is good (Tecno and Foster Associates did

99

111–113

a lot of prototyping), though the theoretical and metaphorical sub-structure woven round this range by Tecno is, unlike the work itself, overstated. The very overstatement, however, serves to raise an interesting general issue about the nature of design, emotion and metaphor.

Tecno says: 'It cannot be said that Nomos is a thing – a collection of tables, an interior decorating system for the office or a plan for the home. It is all of these, of course, but, first and foremost, and basically, it is a way of thinking – of creating the "surface" function in general terms. A flat geometrical place where man has always performed his public and domestic rituals with regard to work, writing, eating, negotiation, prayer, play reading . . . The exhibition [Nomos was first shown by Tecno in Milan in 1986] puts a sampling of these solemnities on display.'

While it is true that Foster has created a system that is – 'moving', that has an emotional content, surely we are not about to kneel at prayer with Tecno? Certainly not. Yet in fact, what we are dealing with in architecture and in design are 'abstract' combinations of shape, mass, form and colour that, properly arranged, can induce a response which may be ecstatic, solemn, quiet, lively. . . . In short, we are dealing with perceptual recipes whose impact is more likely to be biologically than 'spiritually' grounded.

The American painter, Mark Rothko, saw abstract art as a carrier of spiritual value. According to the critic, Suzi Gablik, Rothko claimed that if the spectator read his paintings solely in terms of spatial and colour relationships, then he had failed to understand them. 'You might as well get one thing straight. I am not an abstractionist . . . I'm not interested in the relationship of colour to form to anything else. I am interested in basic human emotions. And the fact that a lot of people break down and cry when confronted with my pictures shows . . . they are having the same religious experience I had when I painted them.'

Rothko may or may not have been a fine painter, but his logic is questionable. The 'basic human emotions' he spoke of are responses to the basic shapes and colours he used – there is literally nothing else there to respond to. The fact that some people weep in a room full of Rothko's paintings is not evidence for religious experience, but is indicative of a perceptual-biological-emotional reaction to a given set of colours and forms, and to a contrived setting. Change the recipe and you will make them laugh. For hundreds of years architects have had recipes for 'manipulating' or directing experience. The art of architecture and design is in discovering and refining these recipes. The modern movement, to which Foster belongs, has given us many new compositions.

But all movements, modern or not, must deal with relevant technology. These days desks house telephones, colour monitors and personal computers. Such needs, as Foster demonstrates, call for an imaginative design that is fluid in its construction to accommodate a client's changing requirements. Electronic communications technology is changing fast and little stability can be expected in this field for some time. Of the few certainties, we may note that the amount of desk-top equipment adds to the heat output; and the obvious consideration is ducting for the cables.

Cable technology, as well as aesthetics, had its part in the design of another new and highly praised office system, called From Nine to Five. It was created by Richard Sapper (West 86–91 Germany) for Castelli (Italy), and was launched at the end of 1986. Sapper's system is visually very powerful, with the most dramatic elements being the central triangular beam from which the work surface is cantilevered. The desking system comes in three variations: Managerial, for senior executives; Operational, for middle management; and Professional, for junior staff.

The triangular beam, the deep drawer unit and the single square leg form an impressively architectural structure, but an important part of their function is to contain and provide easy access to the number of cables required by computers, telephones and printers. The interior of the beam and the leg can take a lot of wiring and in the drawer unit there is a 'cable dump' for taking the larger plugs and feeder cables.

Of course, not everyone agrees that cables must be hidden away. The respected design critic Lance Knobel has argued that although most designers' instincts are for purity of design, the obsession for neatness is arguable: a system that buries the wires in the furniture may need a 'full-time team of "facilities-managers" who make certain that cables are properly positioned and desks never moved without careful preplanning'. Hiding the wires away demands an organizational style which – Knobel says – is fortunately not the style of every office. Thus a loose-fit form of cable management, which may not have the visual precision of a tightly designed scheme, may allow users greater freedom.

Sapper has, like all careful designers, sought out the flaws in existing systems to see what needs correction. He felt that a fault with current office systems was the tendency to put workers facing the wall with their back to the door, thus creating unease and a feeling of vulnerability to people behind them. Thus the standard Sapper configuration is to have the wall behind the desk, so that the worker looks out into the office. Moreover, there is a need to prevent glare from lights and windows falling onto VDU screens, since this is fatiguing for the operator; Sapper's use of back and side partitions cures the problem.

From Nine to Five incorporates certain ergonomic enhancements – the cantilevered work surface can be positioned at one of three heights; the handles on the drawers are made of rubber so that you do not jar your limbs on them, and the key handle is also rubber; the lock to the drawers is to be found on the top of the drawer box, not its end – so that you do not unwittingly knock into it and damage the key in the lock.

Systems are not exclusively for the office and Antonia Astori's work for the Italian company Driade straddles both the office and the domestic market. Her systems storage designs are suitable for the kitchen, for example. Her storage units and work surfaces are stunning. They 109 continue the tradition of De Stijl and are highly practical. Astori is an architect. Her sister-in-law, Adelaide Acerbi, an eminent graphic designer, says that Italian design is successful because it is in the hands of architects: 'Industrial design is like the production of individual sculptures but architecture is the production of systems. It is the difference between having a number of single ideas and developing a whole philosophy.'

Antonia Astori's Oikos and Kaos systems are well known. A limited edition book, published as a celebration of Astori's work, describes the paradigmatic Oikos system as follows: 'The system consists of sectional panels which, fixed together, make up pieces of furniture, fully fitted walls, and interwalls. The basic idea is to provide fixed structures to serve as containers and to define several spaces within the house, and then to grant the user utmost freedom in completing those spaces at will by combining single pieces of furniture of his own choice.' Astori says: 'I like some neo-classicism but I dislike excess. There are references to Palladio in my work. But post-modernism rediscovered the column and I use that even though I do not like the column that much – it was introduced as part of a game.'

When she first launched the Oikos system in 1973 there was no competition; today there are twenty rivals, but Oikos was designed to be updated and it keeps its edge.

Systems furniture for offices and homes depend for their success on accurate technical specifications and good, reliable and durable fastenings and fixings. Astori's technical collaborator is another woman, Fierella Gussoni. Driade's systems furniture is, for the most part, flat packed, and Driade ensures that its sales staff and representatives in stores understand all there is to know about assembling the work.

CHAIRS

Understandably, given that so much design attention in the office and the contract furniture market generally is devoted to the idea of furniture as a serviceable tool, the emphasis tends to be on practical issues. The stackable chair, for example, which is found in offices, conference and lecture rooms, and schools is not an object redolent with metaphor. Nevertheless, attention to the requirements of ease of stacking, light weight and durability has provided two or three design classics. There is, for example, the Kartell 4870 by Anna Castelli Ferrieri discussed in Chapter I.

One of the most successful post-Second World War contract market chairs is the ubiquitous Poly stacking chair, launched in 1963 and designed by Robin Day (UK) for Hille. It uses polypropylene, a plastic invented in Italy in 1954. This plastic was especially suitable for injection moulding and had the right mixture of lightness, durability and flexibility to make a single shell seat practical and commercially viable. The Poly continues to be used all over the world (it has been much copied) and it is used as a fixed seating unit as well as a stacking chair. An equally revolutionary chair, even more so perhaps than the Poly, was Vico Magistretti's Selene chair. Entirely made of plastic, it had a good stacking performance. It was produced by Artemide in 1968.

Even so, new materials do not always provide the best solutions to specific aspects of the brief. Day's Poly chair is an excellent all-rounder and its general toughness and cheapness enable it to stand up to schoolchildren and university students. Its stacking performance does not match that of the most elegant classic in stackable chairs – the Rowland G 40, designed by David Rowland in 1964. This beautiful chair was also launched in an up-dated version called Sof-Tech in 1980. The G 40 is light and uses chromed steel for its frame.

The most technological object in the office is the modern work chair. Indeed, the contemporary office chair is in danger of becoming over-engineered; as an instrument of ergonomics it has attracted as many theories, variations and approaches as childbirth. Very often the development in plastics technology has been crucial to success because much of the give and take in the back rests and arms of these chairs is made possible by plastics that are strong enough not to distort, but pliable enough to give. A tiny number of office chairs seem to have been under-engineered; they have exploded through, it seems, a concatenation of events involving the gas lifts and metal fatigue.

There are several chairs which are good and which (on my brief acquaintance) seem comfortable, but no one can agree which is the best since sitting remains a personal activity. In 1985 Helen Buttery, design journalist, conducted a test survey of eleven office chairs and used as her guinea pigs an architect, an ergonomist, a VDU operator and a product designer. The VDU operator seemed most often satisfied, the product designer least.

Buttery learned the current ergonomic tenet: that there is no correct sitting posture and that it is good for the spine to be in constant movement. So the orthodoxy in office chairs now is a back rest that moves with the sitter. One of the testers concluded that you really needed to learn to sit properly and then you would not need the gimmicks. But because many people do not learn to sit properly, the designer's task is to accept this as one of the 'givens' and design in those very features which are too easily dismissed as gimmicks.

Among the most important designers of office chairs is Mario Bellini (Italy). Bellini's Persona chair owes its basic structure to the concept of the plastic shell – pioneered by Robin Day. The shape of the seat shell and its integrated back rest is such that the back rest widens as you sit down and the seat lowers. Pressure on the seat controls the counter pressure on the back rest – internally there is a sophisticated linkage and balancing system.

Persona's designer and manufacturer state that 'Using the automatic, or synchronous, 120

Left, 40-in-4 stacking chair. David Rowland.   Chromed steel and upholstery.   USA, 1964

Right, Chair. Robin Day for Hille Ergonom.   Polypropylene. UK, 1963

control system in the shell, the sitting position can be altered by movement of weight [your weight as you nestle down] without actually having to adjust the chair.' This may be the answer to the often-made comment that adjustable seats are all very fine but few users ever bother to adjust the chairs or even know how to adjust them. Having required us to think about sitting, designers like Bellini are, sensibly, trying to take the thinking out again in recognition of the fact that some of us are too lazy to find out how the simplest machines work and must be mothered into using them properly.

119   Bellini is also among the first to seek to design a chair which is technologically and ergonomically efficient but which does not look like a machine. His Figura chair is fabric-covered and he has eliminated the levers and buttons that are a feature on many chairs. You simply press the release buttons under the seat and the chair locks into position. It is claimed that this is the first office chair to mould itself to each occupant. However, Figura has some rivals

124, 125   in that claim. The well-known American designer Niels Diffrient, whose Helena office chair has won much praise and several awards in the USA, is quoted as saying: 'I thought I could do a simple chair with a rather vast ergonomic or human factors idea and make it quite good looking. One of my first criteria was that the Helena be a comfortable fit for a wide variety of people. It is a completely adjustable chair.'

Everyone is seeking the world chair. As Emilio Ambasz, architect and designer, remarked: 'The ideal chair would be one that moves automatically with the body as the glove moves with the hand.' We will yet see office workers suspended in warm salt water. Yet the concern with good posture and comfort is, of course, a good thing. It is precisely the kind of service that design should address itself to; the benefits in terms of office efficiency due to physical wellbeing are calculable, for back problems are a major reason for workers taking sick leave. 122, 123 Diffrient has also devised the Jefferson chair, a complete office in itself consisting of a rampantly comfortable chair and footstool with one or two steel columns from which are cantilevered lights, occasional tabletop, micro-computer screen and keyboard. Naturally, wire management is taken care of via the steel columns.

Unlike batch-produced or one-off art projects, the market for office chairs is highly competitive. *Architectural Review* (London) published an interesting analysis of the design development of Marcatre's Air Mail range of chairs (Italy). Designed by Santiago Miranda and Perry King, they also had an important input from production engineer Annabile Mandelli, who wanted a chair that was easy to produce with as few parts as possible. A third designer, Marco Paglioli, was employed to extend the range. This is another example of the office chair as a world chair – a basic concept with many variations tailored for specific countries.

Not everyone is pursuing the high-tech line. As we have already seen in Chapter 2, the Norwegians have taken a natural childbirth approach to furniture. The Balans chair, designed by Peter Opsvik, does make its appearance in offices. Some people found the earlier versions of this chair were not to their taste because it was hard to get in to. Balans has become a credible system of sitting, but outside Scandinavia it is at present too faddy for many offices.

In fact, there will always be a place for elegance, which dispenses with the demands of technology and sociology. One can be very comfortable sitting simply on a wooden stool and although the Archizoom Due (1973) by Paolo Deganello and Gilberto Corretti for Marcatre is 114, 115 demonstrably more sophisticated than a stool, it is much less technological than many work seats and yet comfortable, simple and beautiful to look at.

The office is both a public and a private space: and, even where work is unpleasant, it becomes, through habit, familiarity, and territorial instinct a quasi-domestic activity. Yet, interestingly enough, the need for territorial space is just as acute in genuinely public spaces. And it is in such places – railway stations and airports, for example – that we encounter another form of systems furniture: fixed seating.

Fixed seating has often compromised rather than asserted the individual's need for defensible space. For example, where there are two rows of fixed seats running back to back, it is

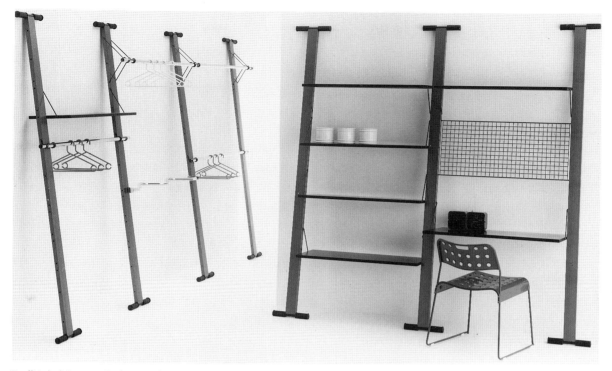

Graffiti shelving, stack chair. Rodney Kinsman of OMK. UK, 1983

important that when the heavyweight male sprawler flops down on the seat behind you, you neither bang heads nor feel your own seat move under his weight. Aircraft seats are notoriously irritating because the 'seat back' position of the person in front violates your space behind, forcing you to become nose to scalp with a stranger.

The fixed seat in a confined space is basically barbarous: its popularity with designers of fast-food restaurants is proof of the fact that the science of fast food is to dissuade clients to linger. Café society, in which men and women huddle into breakaway cliques or congregate into whole ideological movements or simply mass together for a good time, would never have developed on fixed seating. Fixed seating is anti-social and its merits are all in the proprietor's favour, not the customers. Such seats prevent people making the restaurant untidy and they are designed so that it is simple to get a broom and a floor polisher underneath. In truth fixed seating in restaurants or cafés is unwarranted, except for its convenience for cleaners. In aircraft there is no alternative and in aircraft lounges, where there are large numbers of people in transit, it is essential for safety as well as speed of movement for the seats to be kept in order.

One of Norway's leading furniture designers has devised a revolutionary resting place for public spaces. Svein Gusrud has created a tall free-standing plank, complete with leg and arm rest. The plank is at about 80 degrees, so that you lean as you wait. This has great possibilities for banks, airports and railway stations. The one drawback may be aesthetic: row after row of these objects may suggest a landscape of graveyard headstones which would lend an inappropriate metaphor to, say, an airport. Yet they do fulfil the criterion of defensible space. 103–105

One of the most successful public seating arrangements has been devised by the English company Fitch and Co. The Gull Wing seating for the new London Heathrow airport terminal, designed by Peter Crutch, is now produced by Hille Ergonom Ltd. The design is comfortable, flexible, does not rock or yield when other people sit on the other seats, and has the usual benefits of being easy to vacuum beneath. It is one of the more civilized examples of fixed seating. Another example of successful public seating designed by an Englishman is the OMK range by Rodney Kinsman. His work is also manufactured by the Italian company Bieffeplast. 137

My dislike of fixed seating and prejudice against any design which plays up uniformity notwithstanding, it is evident that systems are here to stay because they are convenient and economic. The art, which the designers discussed here demonstrate, is to make systems serve and not dominate. Indeed, the concept in modern systems design, as it is with so much good design of the late 1980s, is synthesis: not so much tempering the corporate with the individual, as seeking to temper individuality with efficiency. There is a considerable difference in emphasis.

Opposite
82 Race office system
Douglas Ball for Sunar Hauserman
USA, 1978
System shown here at Sunar's London
showroom, designed by Michael Graves, USA

83 Focus desking system
    Paul Atkinson for Hille Ergonom
    Light oak veneer
    UK, 1981

84 Solone
    Achille Castiglioni for Marcatre
    Walnut, top polished, aluminium legs,
      cast-iron base
    h. 74 cm
    Italy, 1982

85 Linking system
    Rud Thygessen and Johnny Sørensen
      for Magnus Olesen
    Beech or oak, lino top
    Denmark, 1986

86,87 From Nine to Five
       Richard Sapper for Castelli
       Work surfaces in walnut, oak veneer
       Steel structure, polyurethane paint
       h. 67–76 cm, adjustable work surface
       Italy, 1986

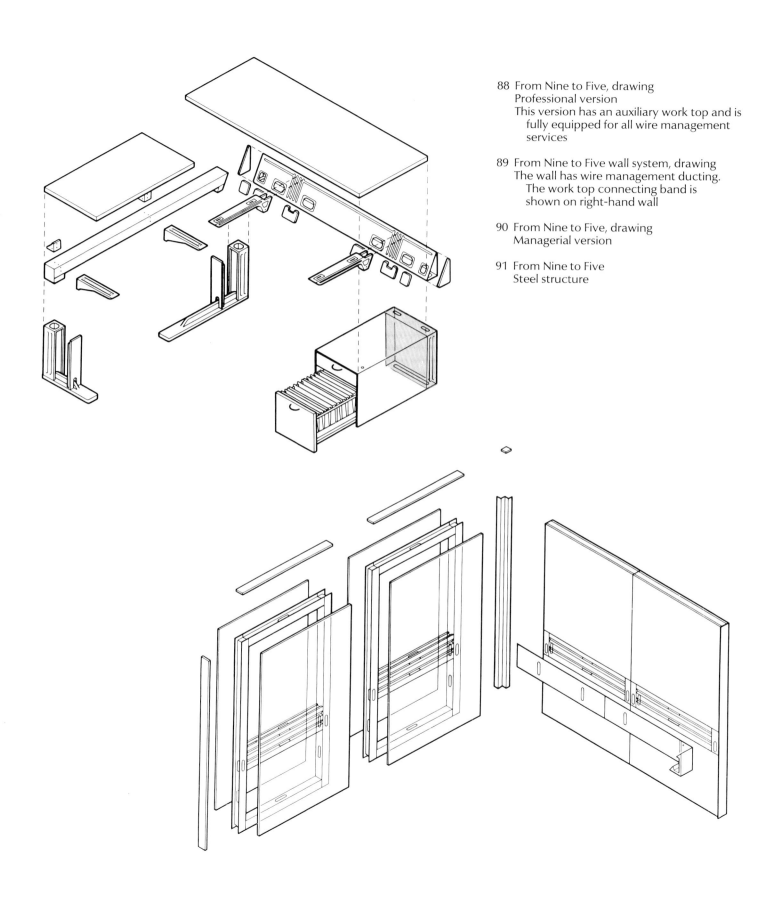

88 From Nine to Five, drawing
    Professional version
     This version has an auxiliary work top and is
       fully equipped for all wire management
       services

89 From Nine to Five wall system, drawing
     The wall has wire management ducting.
       The work top connecting band is
       shown on right-hand wall

90 From Nine to Five, drawing
    Managerial version

91 From Nine to Five
    Steel structure

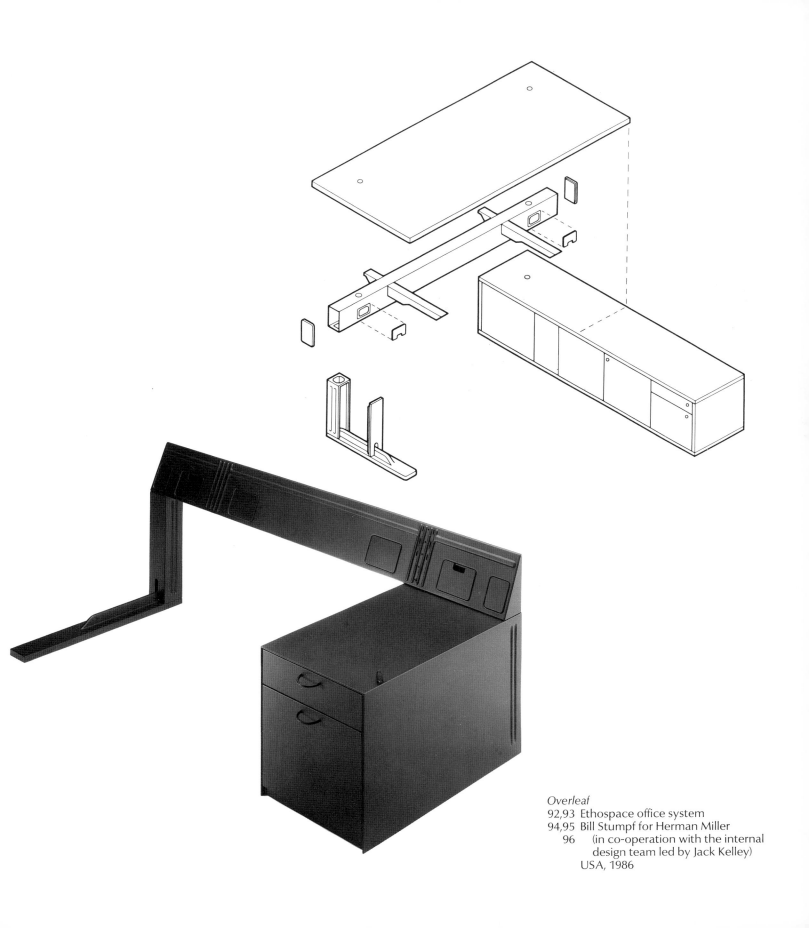

Overleaf
92,93 Ethospace office system
94,95 Bill Stumpf for Herman Miller
  96   (in co-operation with the internal
       design team led by Jack Kelley)
       USA, 1986

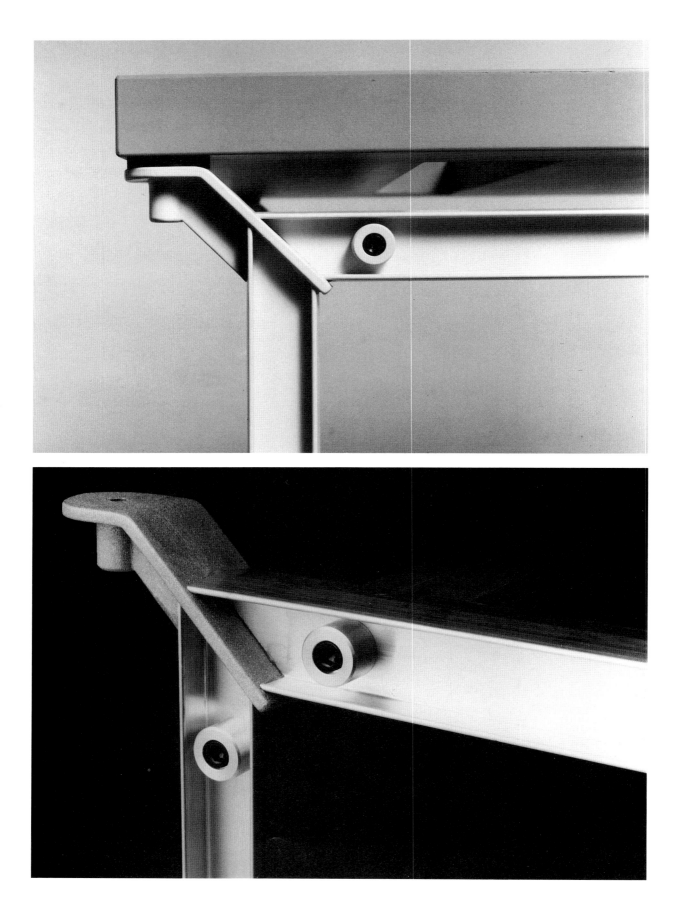

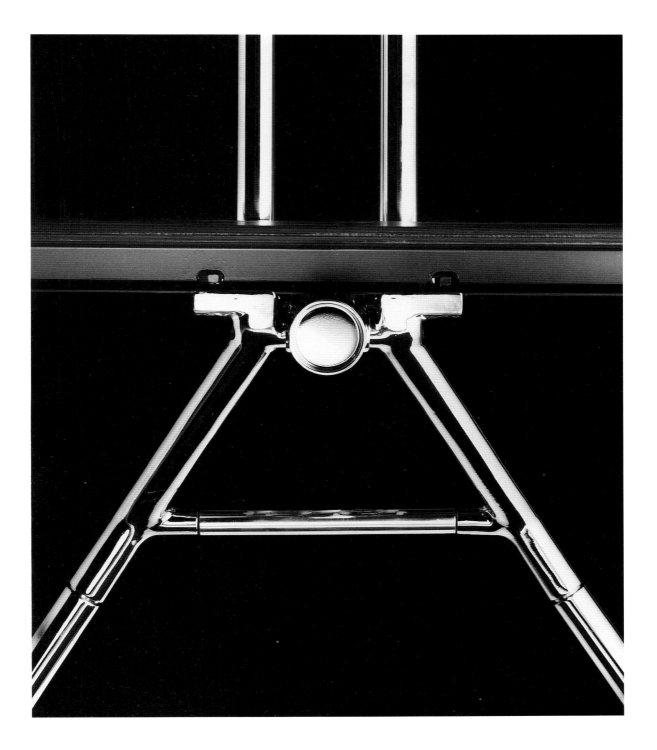

97,98 Prototype desking structure, details
Paul Atkinson
Extruded aluminium
UK, 1985–86

99 Nomos, detail of structure
Foster Associates for Tecno
Chromed steel, adjustable laminate work surface
UK/Italy 1986

100 Solone (Achille Castiglioni)
    Shown here in Marcatre's Glasgow showroom
        designed by Perry A. King and Santiago Miranda
    Scotland, 1986

101 Il Pianeta Ufficio
    Mario Bellini for Marcatre
    Oak-finish panels, laminate work surfaces
    Italy, 1974

102 In-line
   Fred Scott for Hille Ergonom
   Chromed, painted and
      perforated steel
   h. 75 cm
   UK, 1986

103,104 Experiments with seating
   105   in public venues
      Svein Gusrud
      Wood, upholstery
      Max.h. 2 m
      Norway, 1985–86

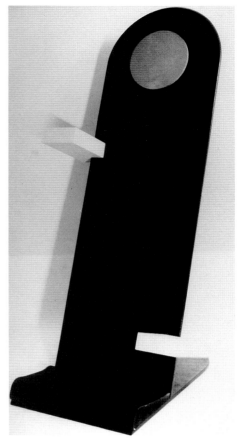

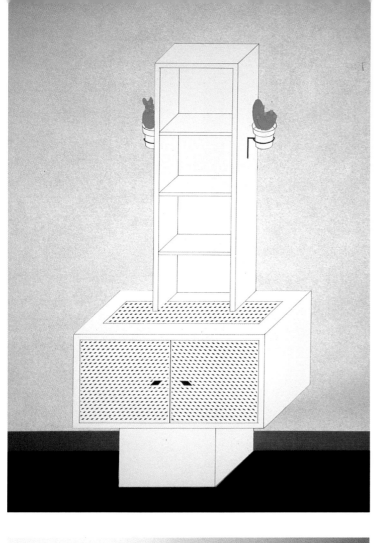

106 Storage unit
Matteo Thun for Bieffeplast
Pressed steel construction
h. 2.09 m
Austria/Italy, 1985

107 Storage unit
Matteo Thun for Bieffeplast
Pressed steel
h. 80 cm
Austria/Italy, 1985

108 Desk, wall storage
Henry Long for Gordon Russell
Japanese sen veneer
h. 73 cm (desk)
UK, 1984

109 Oikos system with fittings
Antonia Astori   for Driade
Compressed wood panels with melamine laminates
h. 2.7 m
Italy, 1972–86

110 Haller system
Fritz Haller
Stove enamel panels, chrome-steel tubes,
   ball connectors
h. 2 m
Denmark, 1960

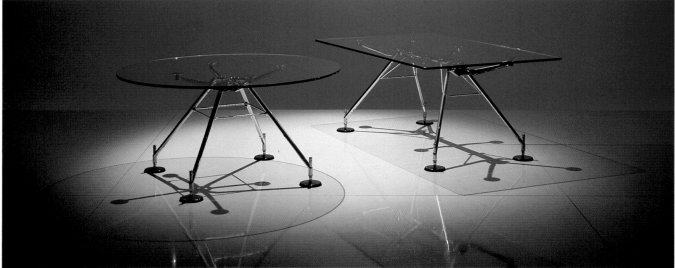

111 Nomos
  Adjustable office desks
  Foster Associates for Tecno
  Chromium-plated steel, plastic laminate
  h. 74 cm (adjustable to drawing-board height)
  Italy/UK 1986

112 Nomos
  Conference tables
  Foster Associates for Tecno
  Chromium-plated steel, glass
  h. 74 cm
  Italy/UK, 1986

113 Nomos
  Detail of the wire management
  design

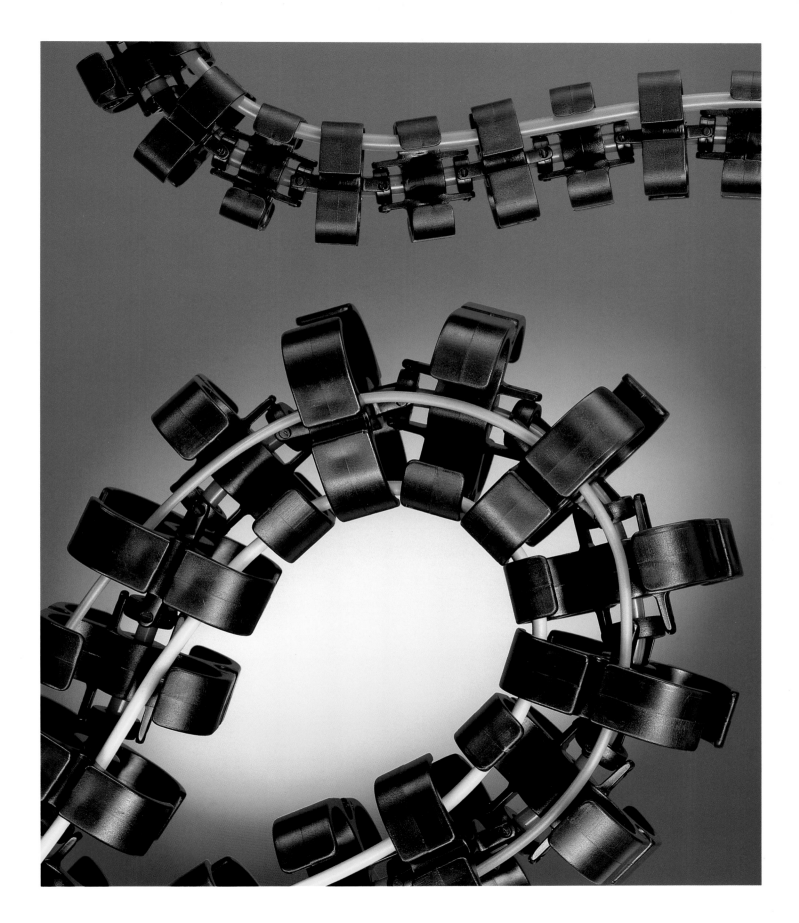

114,115 Archizoom Due
Paolo Deganello and Gilberto Corretti
for Marcatre
Steel, leather
h. 87 cm
Italy, 1973

116,117 Supporto chair
Fred Scott for Hille Ergonom
Aluminium frame, epoxy coated
h. 47–57 cm (seat)
UK, 1979

118 Shape
Peter Murdoch for Hille Ergonom
Lacquered wood
h. 80 cm
UK, 1986

119 Figura
Mario Bellini for Vitra
Steel, fabric covers, plastic shell
h. 41–53 cm (seat)
Italy, 1985

120 Persona
Mario Bellini for Vitra
Steel, aluminium, plastic shell
h. 46–58 cm (seat)
Italy, 1985

121 Basys
Geoff Hollington for Syba
Tubular frame, die-cast aluminium
    base, cold-cure polyurethane
h. 42–50 cm (seat)
UK, 1986

122,123 Jefferson
Niels Diffrient for Sunar Hauserman
Steel, leather
h. 1.20 m
USA, 1986

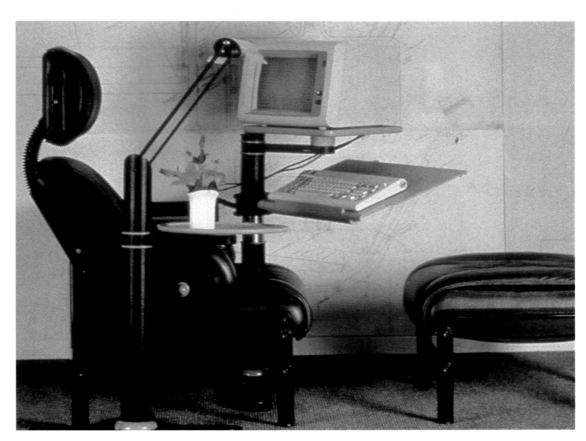

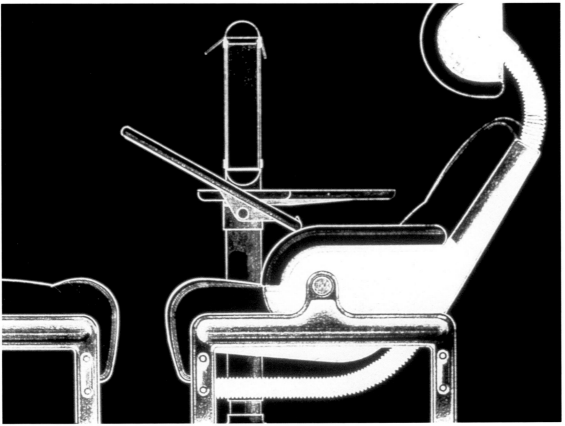

124,125 Helena
         Niels Diffrient for Sunar Hauserman
         Steel, leather
         h. 46–58 cm
         USA, 1984

126   Jobber chair, drawing
         Jane Dillon for Mobilplast
         Steel, plastics, upholstery
         h. 77 cm
         UK, 1982

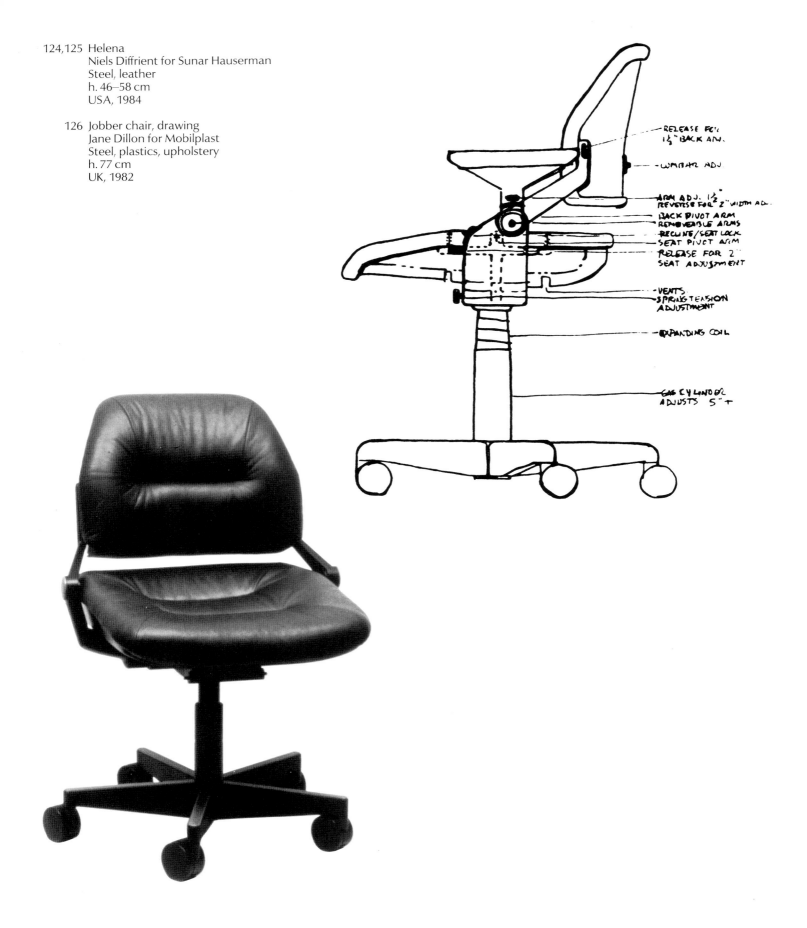

RELEASE FOR
1½" BACK ADJ.

LUMBAR ADJ.

ARM ADJ. 1½"
REVERSE FOR 2" WIDTH ADJ.
BACK PIVOT ARM
REMOVEABLE ARMS
RECLINE/SEAT LOCK
SEAT PIVOT ARM
RELEASE FOR 2"
SEAT ADJUSTMENT

VENTS
SPRING TENSION
ADJUSTMENT

EXPANDING COIL

GAS CYLINDER
ADJUSTS 5"+

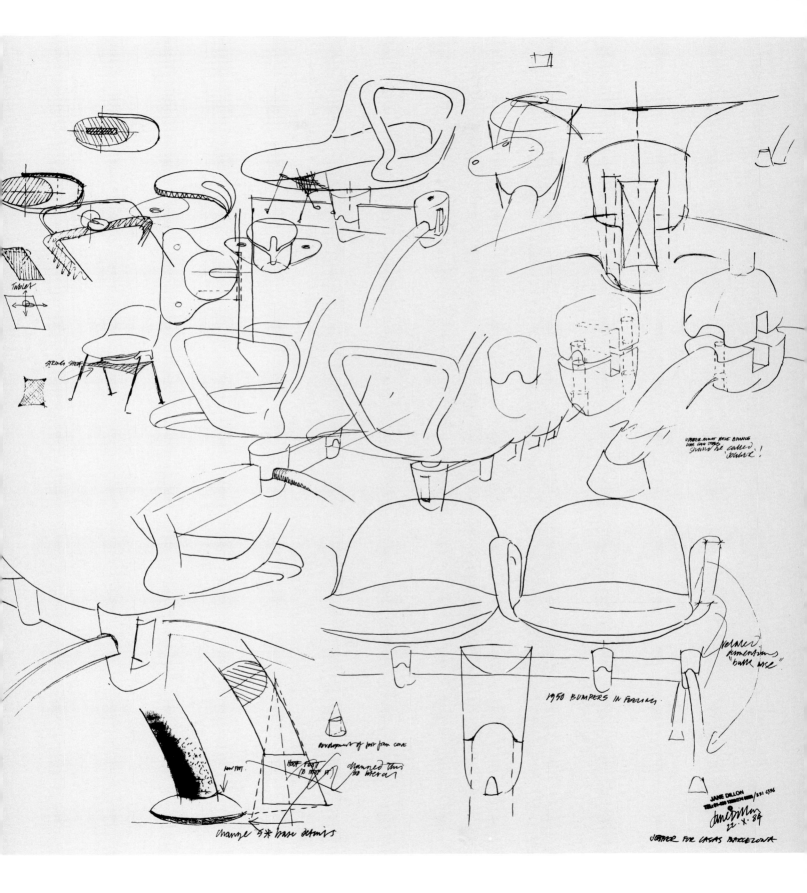

127,128 The Walking Office
129,130 Vincenzo Iavicoli and Maria Luisa Rossi
Consists of keyboard, display unit,
acoustic coupler/cassette recorder
Italy, 1984

131 The Walking Office
Vincenzo Iavicoli and Maria Luisa Rossi
Illustration by Cosimo Megani
Italy, 1984

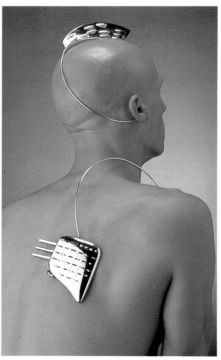

Overleaf

132 Reception desk
Rud Thygesen and Johnny Sørensen
for Magnus Olesen
Beech
h. 1.20 m
Denmark, 1986

133 PA chair
Paul Atkinson for Hille Ergonom
Tubular steel, foam-covered beech
laminate
h. 84 cm
UK, 1985

134 Desking system
Rud Thygesen and Johnny Sørensen
for Magnus Olesen
Beech frame, linoleum top
h. 73 cm
Denmark, 1986

135 Morrison Open Office system
Andrew Morrison for Knoll
International
Steel ribs, fibreglass and
hardboard, 27 finishes
USA, 1986

136 Cameron Office system
Douglas Ball for
Sunar Hauserman
Wood, steel
h. 70 cm
USA, 1983

137 Gull Wing public seating
Peter Crutch (Fitch and Co.)
Cantilevered steel
h. 75 cm
UK, 1985–86

4

DESIGN AS OPPOSITION

Space-age table. Fred Baier.
Laminated wood, plywood, chipboard. UK, 1980

Art, craft and the 'one-off' contribution

Since the 1960s the experimental sector in furniture design has tended to split into two areas — new design and art-craft. I have split this essay into 'Design' and 'Craft' for the convenience of discussion, but I have found it instructive to keep the photographs of the work together. Conceptually, Wendell Castle (USA) and Erik de Graaff (Holland/UK), for example, are far apart, but they stand together in their independence of mainstream design and Main Street marketing-led ideology — it is that independence which everyone in this chapter shares.

NEW DESIGN

A glance through the photographs enables us to make quick but generalized classifications of a familiar art-historical kind. We can see that S. M. Syniuga (West Germany) is in the 20th-century tradition of political art, Floris van den Broecke (Holland/UK) is an example of the modern movement, Ron Arad (Israel/UK) flirts with sculpture, Gerard Dalmon (France) is a surrealist, Danny Lane (USA/UK) is an expressionist, and Sue Golden (UK) nods towards Africa, or rather the imagery of ethnographic collections. In other words, each person is doing his or her own thing apparently outside the normal principles of design or craft, but within the accepted territories of 20th-century art. The work of other designers here is even easier to recognize. Erik de Graaff is an exponent of modern-movement abstraction. Regardless of his intentions we can — like lawyers, and perhaps unfairly — call up precedents for his ideas from De Stijl and the Russian Constructivists. Michael Graves, whose appearance in this section is perhaps 149, 150 disputable given that his designs are marketed by companies such as Sunar Hauserman, is looking towards craft and history. Graves is chosen because he believes he is in opposition to mainstream design. He, or his publicity people, explain that where most modern furniture attempts to be 'overly machine oriented in its associative values, these tables refer both to their anthropomorphic identification of our sitting position relative to them and to the craft technique of both former and present day construction'.

Fine-art or applied-art labels and art-history primers can help us log the work, but we can do more by speculating about the work's intention, to decide whether it fulfils its purpose (and if the purpose was worth fulfilling).

The easiest work to assess ought to be Siegfried Michail Syniuga's, since it has a narrative. Syniuga's seating uses easy-to-recognize imagery, such as the USSR's hammer and sickle and the USA's stars and stripes. The back rest to Syniuga's sofa shows a representation of the two superpowers apparently sodomizing each other. Many people could probably agree about the meaning of this work: the hammer choking in the throat is the repression of freedom by tyranny, or the obliteration of argument by ideology; the sodomizing of America by the USSR could be a nice illustration of the uneasy, or hostile, yet intimate relations between groups of men who horsetrade in power. They have different views but similar mentalities. Different interpretations could be fitted to this work (as critics do when they argue over a novel), yet the area of discourse would be the same. Syniuga's intention might thus be to cause argument.

Part of Syniuga's intention, on the other hand, may rest in making objects so extreme that they catch the attention of the media, but — apart, perhaps, from wanting to make us laugh — the only genuine purpose in making so many of us look at the work is to invite our imaginations to work with his. Indeed, Syniuga invites us to imagine situations where his work would cause a frisson of comment and annoyance — in the Ambassador's office in the Russian Embassy in Washington, D.C. or the American Embassy in Moscow. It would cause offence to some people if they saw it in a Main Street department store window. Moreover, were it to be shown on Main Street, we would see Syniuga's intention more clearly: being a piece of oppositional design, it needs something to oppose — it badly needs the bourgeoisie to be affronted, it needs to upset the members of the moral majority. In fact, it remains corralled as art.

Syniuga is caught out by a contradiction that has trapped other artists living in the liberal West. There artists can more or less do what they want so long as they call it art. What they do is tolerated, except occasionally when the public might be moved by some extreme work to praise or to jeer. However, widespread tolerance often turns to indifference and makes it difficult for an artist to subvert established attitudes. (Naturally, I believe this is a better state of affairs than the other extreme, in which wholesale repression makes every gesture of individuality a bid for martyrdom.) In these circumstances, Syniuga's principal strength stems from the unexpectedness of using a sofa as a vehicle for political satire.

More puzzling, however, than narrative and gestural political art, is work offered as three-dimensional symbolist poetry. Gerard Dalmon (France) and his Sarah chair, presented by the NEOTU gallery in Paris, is an example. Dalmon's Sarah chair, is faintly Egyptian in its form and post-modern in its style, but dressed with ponytails of human hair. It is not viciously unpleasant, but it is curious. Its 'meaning' is a good deal less clear than Syniuga's. Do you even sit on it? It may help to learn that Dalmon had discovered that in the 19th century in Paris there was an outbreak of hair fetishism: men would go out into the streets and cut off the tresses of young women. I like this interesting, darkly attractive chair, but it is so ambiguous that for every hundred people there will be a hundred interpretations.

Many objects are interesting because their authors have given them an unexpected twist. NEOTU, one of Europe's most fascinating modern furniture galleries, has created its special personality by encouraging designers who can take a chair or a table and give it a new life by giving it a shake, like a conjuror. There now, my hat becomes a flag, my flag a table. For instance, look at Epinard Bleu's desk or his Zita table, or the works by Elisabeth Garouste and Mattia 208 Bonetti.

The attraction of NEOTU's furniture is not essentially mysterious: NEOTU-style is composed from the poetry of materials and order versus disorder. Therefore in the Zitta table, where we expect symmetry, we have some symmetry – but not as much as accords with our expectations of a table. We are temporarily thrown. It is like finding that a part of a meal is made from plaster of Paris. Bleu has emphasized the idea of balance by making the legs of the table appear in the wrong place (though not drastically so) and he has underlined the need for balance by weighing down the feet. The smooth table-top sits at odds with the rough legs. The whole thing is a well-judged play on those little recipes to do with form and texture, and on our perceptions of light and heavy, the analysis of which we owe to the Bauhaus art-cooks Johannes Itten and Paul Klee. Our responses to asymmetrical plays with symmetrical objects are probably biologically grounded and part of a common culturally shared response system.

Naturally, apart from shared perceptual responses, there will be more individual responses according to our personal memories and predilections for particular materials. On a personal basis anyone's memory can be triggered by an object: the Zita table might evoke a memory from childhood, of making furniture out of bits and pieces for a den.

Much of NEOTU's work also ploughs the classic 20th-century art tradition of the found object which is then altered. In this case the found objects are all mental ones: they are our preconceptions based on everyday knowledge of what to expect from 'a chair' or 'a table'. But these familiar objects have been picked off from the seashore of expectation and given a twist – just as artists, following in the steps of Picasso, love to do the same with bits of driftwood, scrap metal, bicycle handlebars and so forth. The intention is then to entertain us with the magic of transforming one thing into another.

Some designers bravely ignore the expectations of other people entirely, though, in spite of everything, a few people do like their work. But liking is not the same as understanding. Consider the Dutch designer Erik de Graaff, who lives and works in England. His furniture is the 157–164 antithesis of all Main Street design. Most outsiders, including myself, automatically respond to de Graaff's work by referring it back to designers such as Gerrit Rietveld or artists such as

Kasimir Malevich and Piet Mondrian. De Graaff denies that these individuals are starting points. 'My starting point is the body. For two years before I went to the Royal College of Art I made no furniture – I just drew the body and its seating positions. Then I built myself a room which was 8' by 12' and in this room I began to arrive at seating. But I did not then and I do not now ever want to make compromises. I saw the bare room in relation to the body and I did not see my work as furniture but as a succession of "body tools".' The logic of a body tool is basic: for a body to sit, it needs a plane and a supporting structure, and for the body to sit against something, it needs two planes and a supporting structure.

'I work by setting myself an intellectual objective and then only when the piece of "furniture" adheres to all aspects of the objective do I accept it. Only then do I like it. I can only like something if I really understand it. The idea is the core and if the idea is right and the object fulfils the idea then I come to terms with what it looks like. The X Chair was very important. But after I had done it I could do nothing else for a year. I travelled. I could not justify making another chair. I need to justify everything I do. I have no desire to generate objects for the sake of it.' After a year he began work again.

De Graaff has learned that few people will intuit his intellectual process from the finished objects. He does not like, but has accepted the probability that as soon as his mental object leaves the space he controls, it will be put in settings which are (to De Graaff's eye and mind) inappropriate and even subversive of his object's integrity. De Graaff, on seeing a room in which a client is to put his work, has refused to part with the work. But he insists that he is not a dictator, that he finds the interests of other designers of fascination and that all he is describing vis-à-vis his own work is what matters to him in what he does. De Graaff's integrity, although cross-grained, holds out against a world where compromises are the rule. It may share the intellectual integrity of the early modern movement designers and find a parallel in other 'truthful' disciplines, such as the classical architecture of Palladio or the 19th-century vernacular of the American Shakers.

147, 150   Another Dutch designer, Floris van den Broecke, makes no secret of his debt to, and interest in, Rietveld and De Stijl. But like De Graaff, he is especially interested in the chair as a vehicle for design. In an interview with Alison Britton, an English potter with whom he has exhibited, he explained that the Dutch make a principle out of design, and consistency is the ultimate virtue. Like other Dutch people, he finds flatness beautiful and cherishes the light and the sky, the only natural things in Holland.

Van den Broeke is motivated by the need to define and redefine his own sphere of order; thus his work is not in opposition to mainstream design. He shares the industrial designer's commitment to the values of service, dependability and consistency. His work is too pure for people who find that a certain mess (as long as it is not a subversive mess) is reassuringly human.

The least extreme of the work in this section is that of Louis Mueller (USA), whose furniture 166, 167
makes overtures to abstract sculpture. He is a designer and a metalsmith, and has produced
both furniture and sculpture. Anyone interested in 20th-century design will recognize shades of
Josef Hoffmann in Mueller's work, but it is not pastiche. Nor is it oppositional design except
insofar as it is, like Michael Graves' work, an example of a non-machine, decorative aesthetic.
Louis Mueller opposes the modern movement, but he does so in a manner that flatters and
reassures society; he displays no desire to affront people.

There are younger independent designers, such as Jasper Morrison, who manage to have
elements of opposition, independence and the mainstream. What merits special consideration
is Morrison's particular gift for harmony and composition. He sometimes makes jokes: his
Wingnut chair and his hat stand are lively, animated objects – but their most important feature 181, 183
is that they have a decorative language acquired through observation of what lies round us
now. Morrison has stayed alert to the possibilities for imagery that exist in front of our eyes and
feels no urge to salvage metaphors from literature or past symbolic orders. To this extent he
does us a favour: he is showing us something new.

Yet most individual designers working on their own and trying to make an impact are drawn,
almost inevitably, to create an affront; they are almost drawn to violence. Violence is the most
traditional form of opposition. In this light Danny Lane is interesting because his 'expressionist' 168, 169
work has the ghost of violence in its rough crafted metal and 'broken' glass. But the violence is
artificial and gives a thrill of threat without the actuality of assault: the glass is usually smoothed
off at its 'ragged' edges. It is a kind of designer soft sado-masochism.

Bench. Michael Hurwitz. Painted wenge. USA, 1986

The home of the industrialist and the mermaid. Louis Mueller. Constructed bronze. USA, 1985

Lane's loose-limbed and robust forms fit exactly the same sort of function in a domestic setting as a tasteful assemblage of found driftwood hung on a white wall and lit by spotlights. If a whole house was filled with such debris (however prettily contrived), or filled with the Lane aesthetic, then the result would be confusion and boredom. (The same is not true of all aesthetics – consider the work of Kuramata, Morrison and Mari, for example.) However, an occasional Lane, like a single driftwood *objet d'art*, sets everything else off nicely; here is the well-tested recipe of compare and contrast, and the recipe is also present in Lane's choice of materials – glass versus steel.

An obvious feature of radical furniture is its use of rough materials and rough construction, through which many art-furniture makers seek to oppose current and historically acceptable design mores by ostentatiously rejecting fine craftsmanship. There is a rejection of all conventionally decorated or machine-finished surfaces. By using textures and materials alien to the cushions and armchair softness of the Western home, they taunt us with discomfort and ugliness. Consumer materialism is mocked. In Britain the movement for scrap-metal furniture which looks dangerous to use is partly fuelled by nostalgia: the furniture recalls the bomb-sites of the grey post-Second World War period and even the War itself (for which Britons have an enduring affection).

213, 214   Ron Arad's work is especially interesting. Of all the foreign designers drawn to London in the 1980s (some of whom, like Arad, studied at the intellectual hot house of the Architectural Association), Arad is the man who does not let go of design. He may well surprise or even offend you with his quite brutalist chairs, but they have a logic, are well engineered and structurally look right. They also have a strong allusive element. They feed ideas about ritual and they are part of a tough, futuristic urban landscape. They are to me (but not by Arad's intention) the furnishings for Paul Theroux's novel *O Zone* which, published in 1986, is set a decade or so into the future. Theroux's future exists in a constant tension between ugly chaos and sullen order: that is what I see in Arad's work.

Several younger British designers want to believe in the excitement of chaos offered by an apparent collapse of Britain as a manufacturing power. Collapse implies the disintegration of order, suggesting scope for irresponsibility and its attendant romance. In the early 1980s a group of very young architects in London formed NATO — Narrative Architecture Today. NATO invented several items of post-industrial furniture — raw lumps of concrete, corrugated iron, anything that was broken and abused were recycled without much alteration into furniture. This is the style that Nigel Coates, one of NATO's leaders, was able to take to the restaurant owners of Tokyo, who appreciated it as radical chic which they could use for their interiors.

The progress from oppositional chic to restaurant design reminds us that commerce is intrinsic to design. And yet much of the new design shown here is an art-based adjunct to, and not a replacement for, mainstream activity. Some people dispute this and see a strong commercial future for new design and its independent designers. In 1984 Charlotte Perriand said: 'I think we can anticipate a return to a more primitive form of craftsmanship — not in the sense of going back to the techniques of the past, but a return to smaller scales of operation, making use of all the potential offered by present and future technology. There may still be a need for manufacture on a large scale to meet some needs, but more and more will be produced by individuals, by artisans. The impact on creativity could be enormous, each individual could diversify. . . .'

There are many young individualist designers in Europe and in North America who believe that Perriand is correct. No one (apart from Andrea Branzi) has argued the case more intelligently than Jasper Morrison, and he is worth quoting at length:

Today more than ever the part the designer plays in the scheme of things is confused by the variety of guises and disguises the profession affects. For example, there is the design-group designer who is desk-bound and struggling with his corporate identity crisis; there is the company in-house designer tied by his beard to the company products; there is the designer-maker thinking with his chisels; and there is the freelancer who is confident in his skills and inherited assumptions about design. But, just in the picture, there is the designer-thinker who is not satisfied with any of these roles.

The function of design, seen from a social and economic viewpoint, is to make products more desirable and facilitate their manufacture — and the designer has the skills to do both. He is likely to be fascinated by manufacturing and its processes. But a thoughtful designer, looking at the factories built to produce what he designs, may be struck by their inadequacy to provide their public with anything more than reworkings of designs that have proved saleable in the past.

The designer-thinker – at this stage of his (or her) thoughts is unemployable but for the purpose of clear thinking this has its advantages. It is evident that the notion round which the designer-thinker's troubled mind revolves is that of production. Clearly there can be no design without production (although it does not have to be 'mass production') because without production design becomes something else, often (and confusingly) dressed up as art. It is true that design contains its own art and it can be close to sculpture but nevertheless quite separate.

An important part of the designer's art lies in the solution of its manufacture: the quantity needed for the size of the intended market and the costs involved. The balance of these variables is every bit as important to the art of design as its 'sculptural' content. Indeed, the two aspects are interwoven and to ignore either in the pursuit of the other is to miss the point of designing.

Recently the consumer market has been fragmented: the traditional (mass manufacturing) approach to supplying it has increasingly been replaced by smaller operations, which have quickened the pace of supply and demand to an ever more hysterical consumer market. As a result, the larger companies are forced to update their products more often. This demonstrates that production on a small scale is as valid as any other and it has a potential for growth.

There are now two routes for a designer to take, a short and a long one. The short route solves a design problem set by a fixed brief provided by a manufacturer to enable him to use his existing machinery and skills to increase his sales. Although this route secures the manufacturer's immediate future, in the long run it merely fossilizes his technology. Moreover, it provides the designer with little satisfaction other than cashing in his royalty cheques.

The longer route occurs to the designer with foresight: he builds his own factory, not with bricks, but from the sprawling backstreets teeming with services and processes for materials both common and uncommon to his trade. The thoughtful designer knows full well that while the big-time manufacturers and his more employable colleagues are unaware or disdainful of the afternoons he spends wandering the streets, he has only to make his own living to accomplish more than all of them. Why? Because it is more important to keep those small but enormously useful backstreet businesses alive than to maintain a single large, stagnating producer of hand-stapled, upholstered suites.

Design by the longer route offers an approach with an almost limitless range of materials and ways of treating them. Filed randomly in the designer's mind these materials and methods will surface intuitively and simultaneously to marry, at one blow, all the variables of a products's manufacture with the concept of its final appearance.

The designer who is free (unlike the designer-craftsman fettered by his role as a carpenter or the manufacturer with his factory) can take advantage of the variety of facilities and mix them. A builder sub-contracts because he knows he will get a better result than if he asks a bricklayer to do the plumbing. In the same way the new designer or (indeed) the new manufacturer, taking advantage of the multiplicity of skills available, can design and produce with a versatility that cannot be matched by a single factory.

NEW CRAFT

The roots of the contemporary craft-orientated furniture producers are in the late 19th-century arts and crafts movements which were influental in both Europe and the United States of America. Perhaps the contemporary craftsman is less abashed by his or her dependence upon rich clients than the idealists of the late 19th century (who, none the less, in their time succumbed to the commissions of the rich).

Wood is the heart of craft furniture and in the USA the woodcraft movement is spectacular both in the number of people who practise it and in the richness of the work. The founding priest of the modern American woodcraft tradition is Wharton Esherick (1887–1970), whose home and studio in Pennsylvania is an extraordinary design and construction in itself: it has something of the quality of a cubist version of Dr Caligari's cabinet, designed for a boat but tempered with a strong taste for the organic.

After the Second World War, the American woodcraft furniture movement was consolidated by George Nakashima, Bob Scottsdale, Tage Frid, Sam Maloof, Arthur Carpenter and

Far left
Music stand. Wharton Esherick.
Walnut and cherry. USA, 1960

Left
Wagon wheel chair. Wharton Esherick.
Wheel rims and shafts of a cart.
USA, 1931

Cabinet. Tage Frid.
Honduras mahogany. USA, 1982

James Krenov. For many years, as Helen Drutt — one of America's shrewdest observers of American craft has explained — the American woodworker chose to work wood because of the independent way of life it offered. Craft work and the craft life added up to a moral activity. In recent years, Drutt observes that the emphasis has changed. The craftsman, like the designer, seeks the status of an artist.

America places a high value on visible virtuosity and the leading virtuoso in craft furniture is Wendell Castle, whom many people acclaim as an artist. Castle's work interests many Europeans because he represents the conceptual gap between European and American thinking in design-related matters. In Europe the tendency is to view furniture design as architecture writ small: the heart of architecture as an intellectual enterprise is understanding how to construct volumes that satisfy, inside and outside, or intuition of three dimensions. A monumental building and a monumental mass, like a mountain, differ in that the one articulates space, the other sits in it. Wendell Castle's fascinatingly grand pieces, such as his 195 Egyptian desk (1982), exist as discrete objects and sit in but do not use space. And with a mixture of eclecticism and precious materials, used for their own, innate beauty, Wendell Castle has frequently contrived objects that exist not only out of space but out of time. Like Disneyland, they are fantasies.

Castle's early work is pneumatic in its organic swellings and undulations – his seats were either womblike or monuments to the all-American breast. Then Castle went through a period of figurative sculptural work in which he carved hats and jackets lying on or hanging off chairs – the skill shown in this *trompe l'oeil* phase was extremely impressive. I believe, too, that such 194, 196 work is expressive of a particular and recurrent cultural obsession with consumerism and materialism. Every now and again, whenever a society is doing very well materially, a celebration of materialism flowers: look at 17th-century Dutch painting, for example – a celebration of the good life by and for the merchant classes.

In its emphasis on rich woods and creamy anatomy, much American craft movement furniture is a flight of ecstatic materialism. Such flights have their parallels elsewhere in the world: Ferdinand Porsche's design studio and his 84 S recliner is an example, and West Germany most nearly rivals (after Japan) America's luxuriance in material things.

In 1982 several of the leading American furniture craftspeople were invited by the Formica Corporation to design furniture using, in whole or in part, Formica's Colorcore, the name which Formica had given to the newly developed solid laminate in which the colour goes right through (it is like having planks of solid wood saturated with colour). Colorcore can be cut, etched, sawn, routed and layered.

Settle. American Shakers. Beech. USA, *c.* 1850

Writing table and chair.
John Makepeace. UK, 1986

Formica wanted to fix its brand name Colorcore in the public's mind so that it became associated with the material (just as Formica came to mean any plastic sheet regardless of who manufactured it). One of Formica's strategies was to commission well-known designers to produce work and then exhibit it round the world in prestigious galleries. The first Colorcore exhibition, called 'Surface and Ornament', included Stanley Tigerman (USA) and Rodney Kinsman (UK) among its participants. The Colorcore exhibition titled 'Material Evidence' – new color techniques in handmade furniture – included work by Wendell Castle and fellow Americans Judy McKie, Gary Knott Bennett and Mitch Ryerson. Both exhibitions were timely in that they capitalized on the early-1980s fashion for post-modernism and ornamentalism. Formica's intelligent marketing strategy appears to have paid off: Colorcore is to the laminate what Hoover is to vacuum cleaners.

201

199

187–189

197

This has all encouraged the notion of art furniture. However, unlike the work of designers such as Ron Arad or Alexander Fischer (Switzerland) or Gerard Dalmon or Andrea Branzi, the art furniture of Castle *et al.* does not usually seek to comment on the nature of furniture or society's use of it. Art furniture, American style, is not subversive – it is affirmative. It does not want to slap the merchant class about the face; it invites that class to buy work and commission more. Art furniture is a commercial activity, new design is not (new design rather too frequently subsists on teaching, grants and museum purchases).

The affirmative nature of American craft design is rooted in the nature of the materials used and the impressive skill that is employed. It is also paralleled to a degree by some craftsmen in

Britain – most notably John Makepeace, who established his now world-famous school for craftsmen in wood in 1977. Others, including Wendell Castle, have since established schools of their own. Makepeace and Castle share a similar taste for the organic. Neither man is capable of subversion and we can see why: they are makers and entrepreneurs. Specifically, it is unrealistic to suppose that someone can commit himself to lovely materials and a thousand hours of labour and be a subversive or even a questioning designer. Some people see this as the achilles heel of craft. As Jasper Morrison, who is highly sceptical about handicraft furniture, has observed: 'Poor materials imaginatively applied can make a product more desirable than a design which relies on rich materials.' Morrison believes that contemporary craft decoration and elaborate handwork has no meaning and has no role in contemporary design. 'The wasted hours spent in achieving craft decoration are either deducted from the time spent designing or reflected in the final price of the artefact or both.'

There are American exceptions – one of them is the artist Mark Burns, who makes furniture   138
and also makes furniture sets. He and a friend have built up a large collection of 1950s American kitsch work that is full of urban metaphor, Hollywood fantasy, unfulfilled promises. Burns recognizes that seen *en masse* much that he has collected is frightening – he believes this is because many of the plastic or plaster ornaments display a desperate irrationality.

Burns' own work is not irrational, but it can be disturbing. It sometimes shows a preoccupation with physical and mental pain. In one table-cum-lamp owned by Helen Drutt, who is perceptive enough to understand and proselytize Burns' work, there is a beehive on fire. A hand seeking either to get the honey, or save the bees, is nailed. The imagery is at once horrific and kitsch. It is a metaphor for denial.

A commitment to or scepticism about craft depends on one's attitude to the craft ideology: handmade implies good workmanship, which entails integrity, which equals a good deal for the customer. The good deal is further enhanced by the fact that the object is likely to be unique.

However, the word 'craft' has several meanings – it does mean skill, but it also means deceit; and the difference between being a craftsman and being crafty is obvious. From time to time, and in this century most notoriously by architect and writer Adolf Loos (1870–1933), ornament has been despised partly on the grounds that it is deceitful and covers something up. It is obvious why the Shakers, the Quakers and puritans of all kinds – including designers in the modern movement's vanguard – wanted unadorned furniture: ornament and an agitated tampering with the surfaces can be used, like a mask, to disguise bad workmanship. The act of good workmanship is a moral contract: at its simplest it is one person making something for another person and not wanting to let him or her down.

There are several contemporary examples of good plain workmanship combined with non-flamboyant design that seek to keep faith with the craft ideology. Richard Kagan (USA), Alan   220, 222

Table. James Schriber.
Purpleheart. USA, 1983

211, 212   Peters (UK), Robert Williamson (UK) are all plain men, each upholding the virtues of craft, as also
191, 185   do makers such as Jere Osgood (USA) and James Schriber (USA). Osgood has succeeded in
marrying the American love for the organic aesthetic with restraint and superb but not show-
off workmanship. Schriber carries this restraint even further and keeps faith with a basic tenet of
craft ideology – allowing a material to speak for itself. Richard Kagan is an example of a
thoughtful designer determined to uphold the moral contract between maker and client, and
unwilling to let ego dominate either the design or the construction of his work. The same, I
believe, holds true for Alan Peters and Robert Williamson. Of course, whether one likes each
individual piece is a matter of taste – once, that is, the criteria of function, appropriate design,
appropriate materials and fit workmanship have been satisfactorily fulfilled. What I think links
each man is the simple fact that his work is intended for use. Utility is a good taskmaster.

However, the most taxing issue in assessing either new design or current craft is the matter of
'when is it art?' First we have to distinguish between narrative and abstract visual art. In
narrative art we expect an artist to show us what he or she has discovered about some aspect of
human nature or the material world by using either metaphor or superb description. For
example, Pablo Picasso's famous series of etchings of a woman in grief adds to our perception of
what grief feels like because Picasso creates a powerful visual metaphor in which the tears drive
upwards into the eyes like shrapnel.

Abstract art, however, simply is. It just exists, it is itself, complete and there for all to see. You
might almost as well ask what a tree means as to ask what a Jackson Pollock means. This,

incidentally, puts most abstract art very close to decorative art: the two, as decorative artists such as potters and weavers point out, are virtually interchangeable. There is no point in asking what a pot or a chair means, because such objects are self-referential.

Now, with regard to furniture, very little craft and only some new design is art in either the metaphorical or descriptive senses (exceptions here include S. M. Syniugua). For a furniture maker to make a comment or provide a description about an aspect of furniture, say the social role of the armchair, he or she must create something that distances itself from real armchairs. Andrea Branzi might be doing this with his work. But furniture can be like abstract art and it can 218 put the formal composition of shape, form, colour and textures as its priority. If it does so, by making the aesthetic composition the priority, it will inevitably demote design considerations such as function and production. Consequently, while art puts aesthetics first, design balances aesthetics with utility.

Of course, descriptive or metaphorical art can easily be banal; it can be bad art and the truth that the artist has discovered may be empty. Indeed, it is dangerous for furniture makers to start building in metaphorical or descriptive content to their work, though some do try. It is dangerous because they are then inviting comparison between their work and that of the best art in narrative sculpture and painting. Nevertheless, we are invited to judge Wendell Castle's coffee table for Colorcore as an attempt at narrative art. The Colorcore catalogue says this: 199 'Wendell Castle's "Coffee Table" stretches the notion of function to its most ceremonial. The cup of coffee, which Castle observes as an American ritual, is given its own shrine here.' Does Castle succeed? That depends on whether you consider the content worthy of the elaboration. Oddly enough, the craft criterion – is it well-made or not? – hardly comes into the matter of metaphorical art. One prefers things well made rather than not in art, but quite often bad craftsmanship (look at the ugliness of Edward Hopper's or René Magritte's brush strokes) does not stand in the way of it being successful. S. M. Syniuga's work is neither enhanced nor diminished by fine craftsmanship, whereas Castle's Egyptian desk, which is neither metaphorical nor descriptive but ornamental, depends for its impact almost entirely upon the craft skill.

Essentially furniture is about design and function, but one is always indebted to the individuals who experiment and innovate, and do what orthodoxy maintains is irrational. In their hands and minds exists our future delight.

Opposite
138 Installation showing beehive lamp and stand
Mark Burns
Wood, clay, matchsticks
h. 99 cm
USA, 1975

139,140 Bureau
Gunther Münch
Lacquered wood
Shown open, then closed
h. 1.8 m
West Germany, 1984

141 Bureau, open, with chair
Gunther Münch
Painted wood
h. 1.5 m
West Germany, 1984

142 Bureau, closed
Gunther Münch

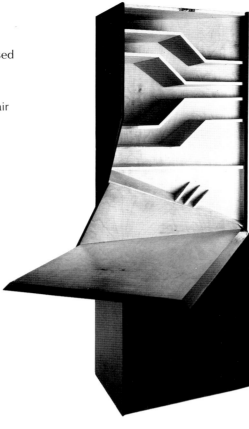

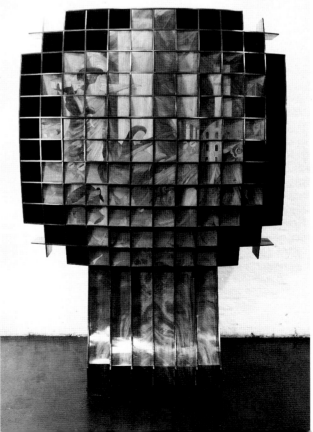

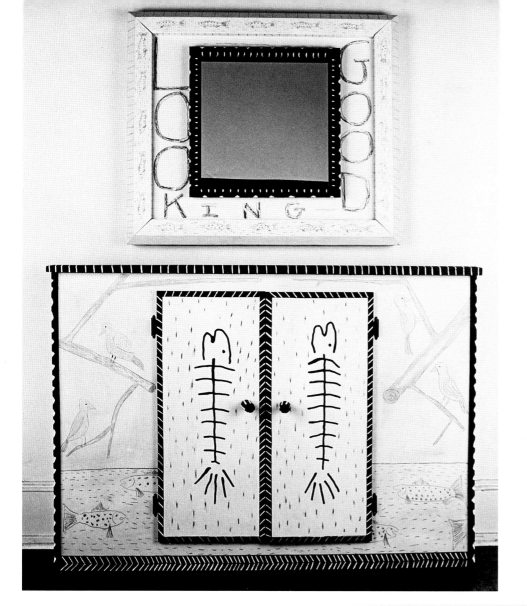

143 Looking Good
      Richard Kooyman
      Wood, carved and painted
      h. 97 cm (chest); 80 cm (mirror)
      USA, 1986

144 Looking Good
      Chest, doors open

Overleaf
145 Pelicans with tassles and
          Dignity no. 1
      John Malcolm Webb
      Aluminium
      h. 1.5 m
      UK, 1984–85

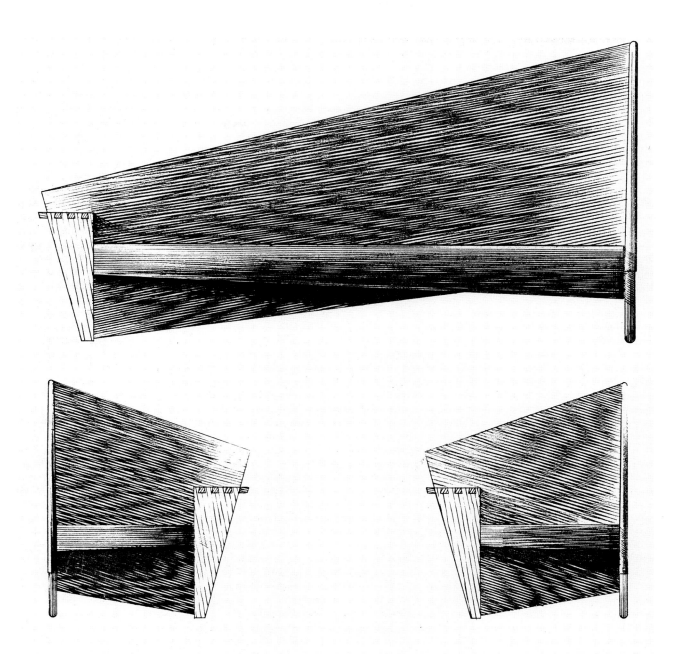

DESIGNS FOR A SETTEE AND TWO CHAIRS   FLORIS VAN DEN BROECKE 85-86
COMMISSIONED BY EASTERN ARTS FOR RECEPTION AREA IN CHERRY HINTON HALL

146 Nadelkissen
Bettina Wiegandt and Manuel Pfahl
Montage
West Germany, 1984

147 Settee and two chairs, drawing
Floris van den Broecke
Holland/UK, 1985–86

148 Side table and chair
  Michael Graves for
    Sunar Hauserman
  Polyurethane finished
    hardwood
  h. 73 cm, 75 cm
  USA, 1984

149 Lounge chair
  Michael Graves for
    Sunar Hauserman
  Hardwood frame, bird's eye
    maple veneer
  h. 95 cm
  USA, 1984

150 Settee, drawing
  Floris van den Broecke
  Wood, foam-rubber upholstery
  h. 85 cm
  Holland/UK, 1985

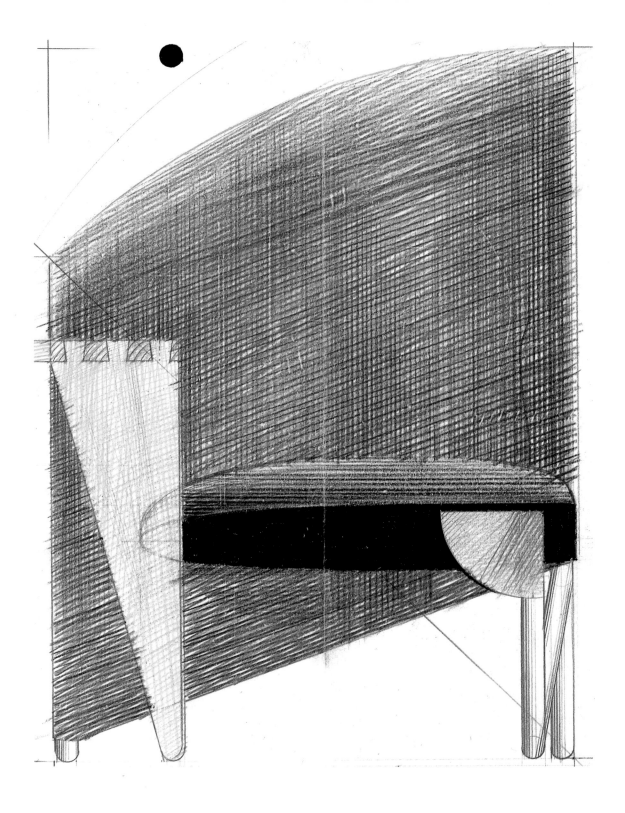

Overleaf 151 Chaise longue
Alexander Fischer
Wood, textured textile
h. 1.2 m
Switzerland, 1985

152 Table
Alexander Fischer
Wood, steel
h. 75 cm
Switzerland, 1986

153 Drawer towers
Alexander Fischer
Wood, steel
h. 2.28 cm
Switzerland, 1983, 1985

154 Chair
    Sue Golden
    Carved wood, painted aluminium
    h. 1 m
    UK, 1986

155 Chair, table, light
    Sue Golden
    Carved wood, aluminium, glass
    h. 90 cm
    UK, 1986

156 Sarah chair
    Gerard Dalmon
    Wood, hair
    h. 75 cm
    France, 1986

157,158 High armchair
   159 Erik de Graaff
       Medium-density fibreboard,
         grey lacquer, steel frame
       h. to arm 65 cm
       UK, 1980–86

160,161 Low armchair
       Erik de Graaff
       Medium-density fibreboard,
         grey lacquer, steel frame
       h. to arm 22.5 cm
       UK, 1980–86

162 Cross chair
    Erik de Graaff
    Black ash or grey lacquered ash
    l. 75 cm (seat); l. 1.2 m (back)
    UK, 1980–86

163, Long armchair
164 Erik de Graaff
    Medium-density fibreboard,
      grey lacquer, steel frame
    h. to arm 22.5 m
    UK, 1980–86

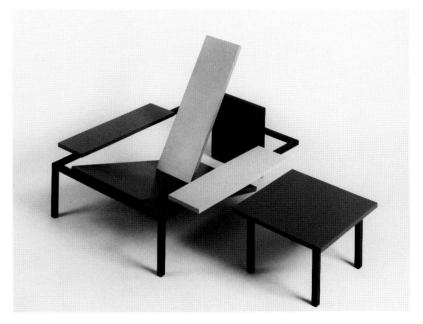

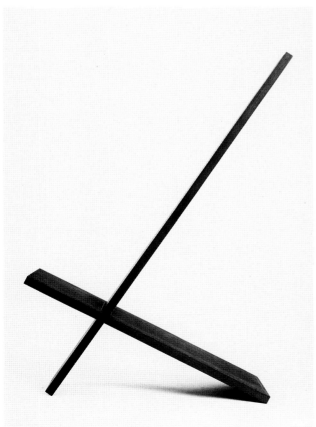

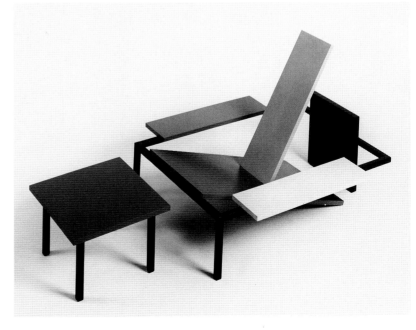

165 Bureau
   Epinard Bleu
   Glass, lacquered metal
   h. 75 cm
   France, 1984

166 Table
   Louis Mueller
   Glass, bronze
   h. 77 cm
   USA, 1985

167 Table
   Louis Mueller
   Glass, bronze
   h. 78 cm
   USA, 1985

168 Table
   Danny Lane
   Etched and sandblasted glass, iron
   h. 70 cm
   USA/UK, 1985

169 Table
   Danny Lane
   Etched and sandblasted glass
   h. 50 cm
   USA/UK, 1985

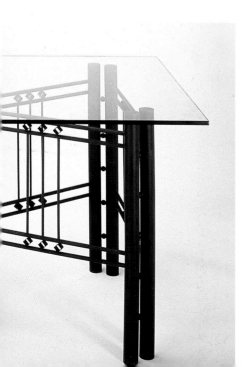

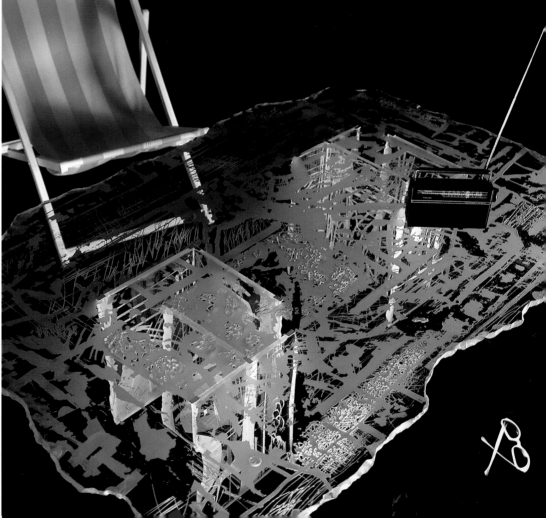

170 Chaise Barbare
   Mattia Bonetti and
      Elisabeth Garouste
   Cast iron, horse leather
   h. 1.18 m
   France, 1981

171 Chair
   Sam Maloof
   Black walnut
   h. 75 cm
   USA, 1950–86

172 Domestic Animal
   Andrea Branzi
   Planed and unplaned wood
   h. 75 cm
   Italy, 1985

173 Quasi-traditional
      Mexican chair
   Anonymous
   Wood, leather, reed
   h. 80 cm
   Mexico, 1986

174,175 Moody chair
   176 Eleanor Wood for Hoskins
      Steel tube frame; arms can
         fold back
      Rosewood feet and hands;
         detachable knitted Rothko
         cover
      h. 70 cm
      UK, 1985

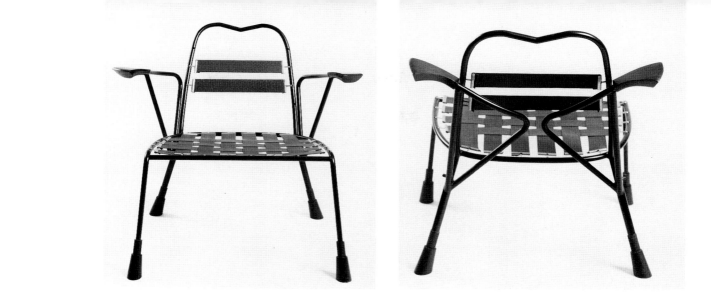

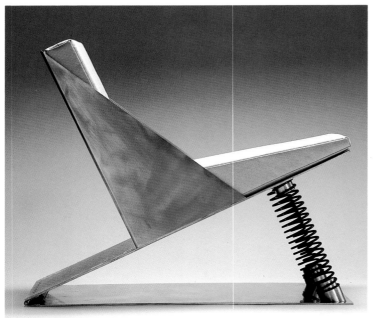

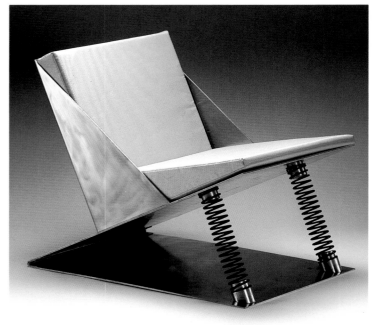

177 Chair
André Dubreuil
Metal bar
h. 75 cm
France/UK 1985

178,179 Rescue Seat
Hermann Waldenburg
Steel, upholstery
h. 75 cm
West Germany, 1986

180 Megatron
Fred Baier
Bent plywood, painted
h. 1.8 m
UK, 1986

181 Hat stand, trolley
Jasper Morrison
Steel
h. 1.8 m, 73 cm
UK, 1986

182 Dining chair and table ·
Jasper Morrison
Steel, plywood
h. 75 cm, 70 cm
UK, 1986

183 Chairs
Jasper Morrison
3 mm aero ply (left)
Hardboard, piano hinges,
   wingnuts (right)
h. 73 cm
UK, 1984

Overleaf
184 Hotel Ukraina chair, sofa
Siegfried Michail Syniuga
Iron, leather, steel
h. 1.80 m
West Germany, 1985

Rocket table,
Herbert Jakob Weinand
Steel, glass
h. 95 cm
West Germany, 1984—85

185 TV/Stereo cabinet
James Schriber
Pickled white oak, perforated metal
h. 90 cm
USA, 1986

186 Conference table
James Schriber
Paduk, leather
h. 75 cm
USA, 1985

187 Fish chest
Judy Kensley McKie
Lacewood, maple, wenge
h. 1.5 m
USA, 1983

188 Fox and Lizard table
Judy Kensley McKie
Carved and painted birch
h. 75 cm
USA, 1985

189 Leopard couch
Judy Kensley McKie
Mahogany
h. 71 cm
USA, 1983

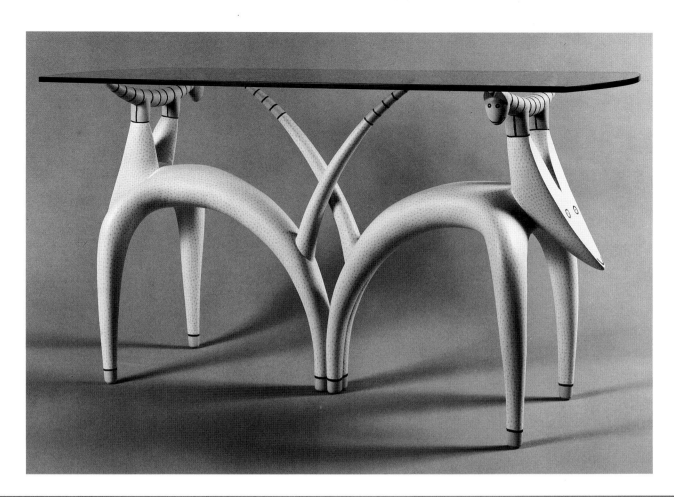

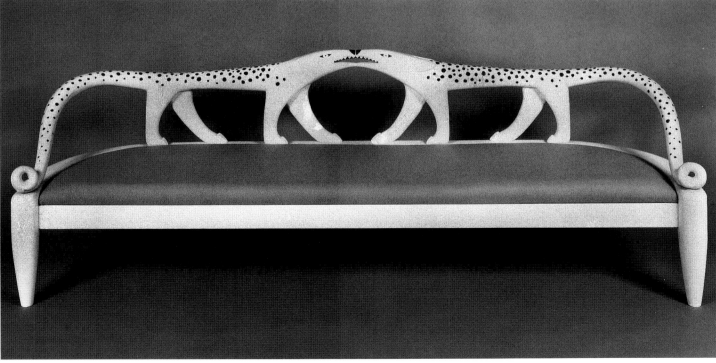

190 Star dining table
     Howard Werner
     Curly maple
     d. 1.60 m
     USA, 1985

191 Desk
     Jere Osgood
     Bulinga top, ash
     h. 73 cm
     USA, 1982

192 Chair
     Dick Wickman
     Blistered maple, colorcore, brass
     h. 81 cm
     USA, 1985

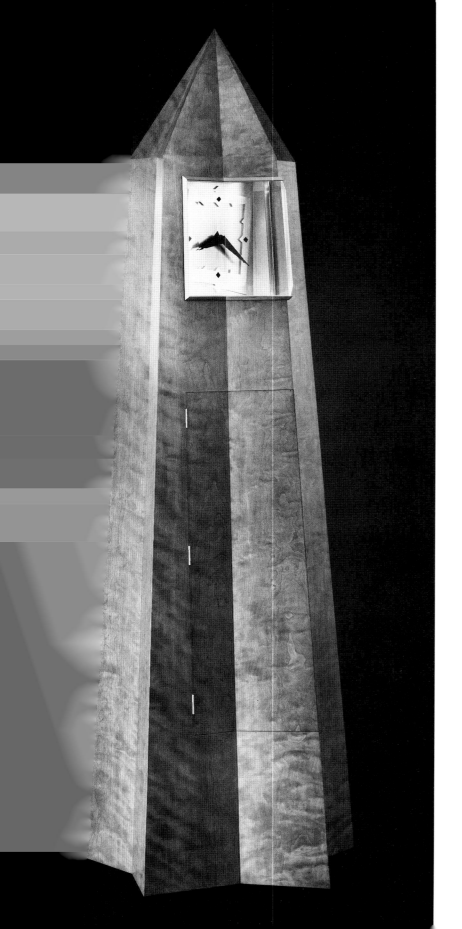

193 Dr Caligari
   Wendell Castle
   Curly cherry veneer, ebony details
      on interior, gold-plated brass
   h. 2.6 m
   USA, 1984

194 Pair of Chippendale chairs with
      smashed hat
   Wendell Castle
   Swiss pear, carved
   h. 90 cm
   USA, 1980

195 Egyptian desk
   Wendell Castle
   Ebony, maple, leather
   h. 75 cm
   USA, 1982

196 Ghost clock
   Wendell Castle
   Bleached mahogany, carved
   h. 2.17 m
   USA, 1985

197 Hall piece
Mitch Ryerson
Colorcore, white oak, iron, mirror
h. 1.5 m
USA, 1984

198 Time is Money clock
Edward Zucca
Painted wood, dollars
h. 1.8 m
USA, 1986

199 Coffee table
Wendell Castle
Colorcore, cherry, ceramic cup
h. 45 cm
USA, 1984

200 Table with still life
Paula Winokur
Clay
h. 75 cm
USA, 1986

201 Tête-à-Tête
Stanley Tigerman
Colorcore
h. 1 m
USA, 1983

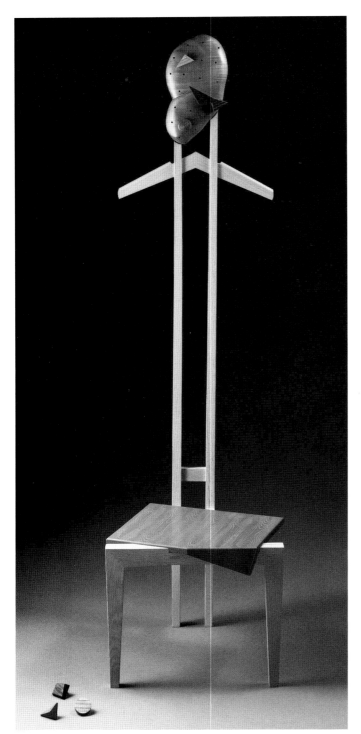

202 Potato Head
   Alphonse Mattia
   Ash, sycamore
   h. 1.8 m
   USA, 1985

203 Face
   Alphonse Mattia
   Ash, sycamore
   h. 1.8 m
   USA, 1985

204 Seat
   Neil Austin
   Laminated wood
   h. 45 cm
   UK, 1985

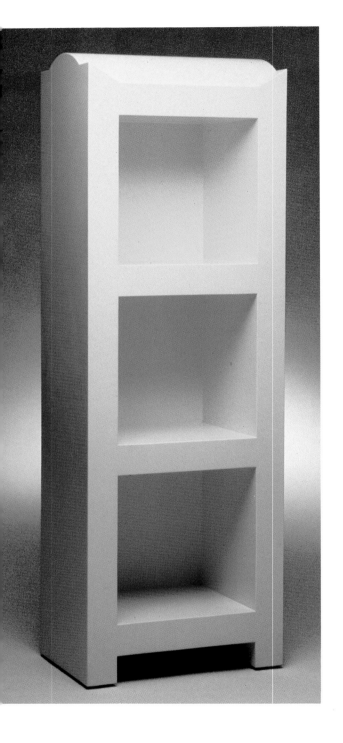

205 Zenith Container
     François Bauchet
     Lacquered wood
     h. 1.8 m
     France, 1982

206 PI chair
     Martin Szekely
     Black epoxy-coated metal, leather
     h. 80 cm
     France, 1984

207 Gueridon Cub House
     Epinard Bleu
     Metal, serpentine marble
     h. 64 cm
     France, 1984

208 Zita table
     Epinard Bleu
     Aluminium, wood, coloured glass
     h. 118 cm
     France, 1985

209 Cabinet
   Alan Peters
   Wych elm
   h. 1.25 m
   UK, 1984

210 Bench
   Jim Partridge
   Oak
   h. 44 cm
   UK, 1986

211 Dining chair
   Alan Peters
   Sycamore
   h. 95 cm
   UK, 1979

212 Side table
   Alan Peters
   Burmese hardwood, sycamore
   h. 76 cm
   UK, 1983

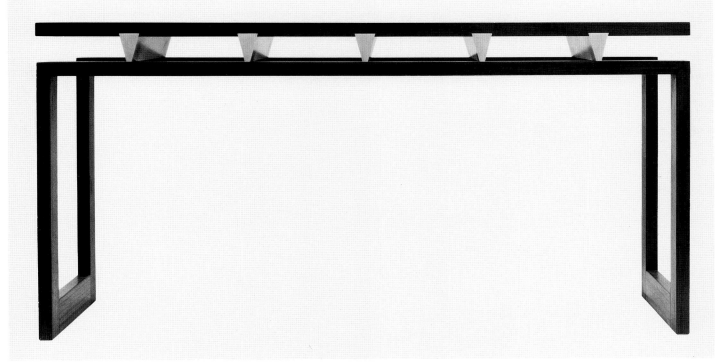

213 Horn chair
Ron Arad
Aluminium
h. 1 m
Israel/UK, 1986

214 Horn clock
Ron Arad
Folded and welded metal
h. 1.80 m
Israel/UK, 1986

215 Chair
 Martin Szekely
 Steel
 h. 75 cm
 France, 1985

Overleaf

216 Steel chair
 J. Tiesteel
 Nickel-plated steel
 h. 80 cm
 UK, 1986

218 Domestic Animal
 Andrea Branzi
 Planed and unplaned wood
 h. 2 m
 Italy, 1985

217 Steel stools
 J. Tiesteel
 Folded and welded steel
 h. 80 cm
 UK, 1986

219 Table
 Ron Arad
 Folded and welded sheet metal
 h. 75 cm
 Israel/UK, 1985

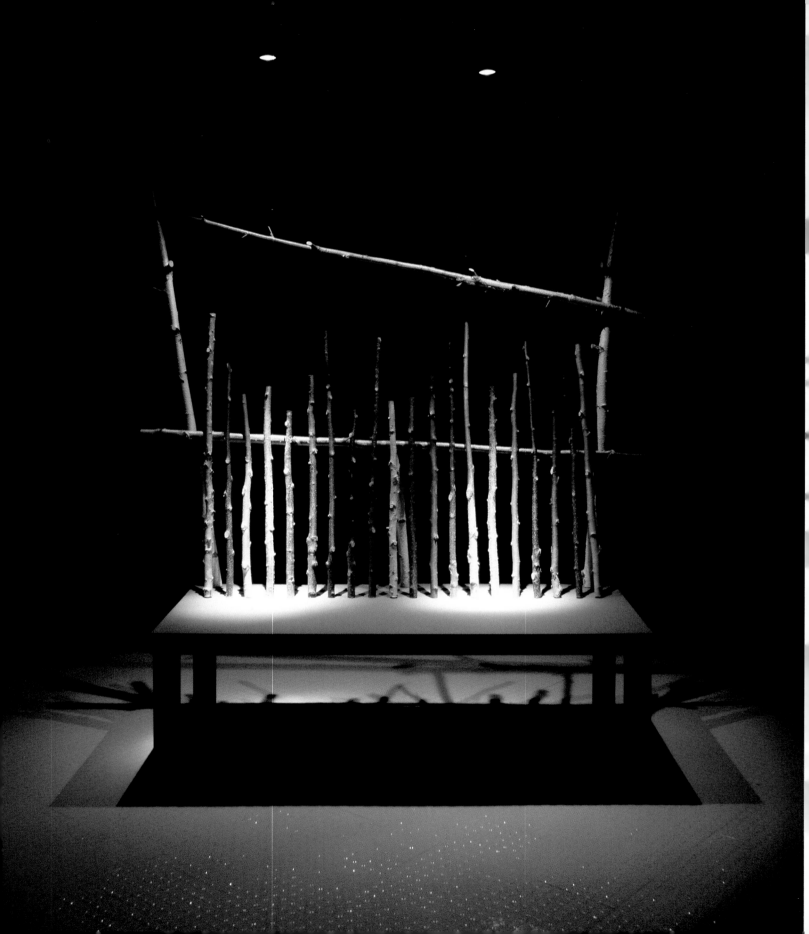

220 Lectern
    Richard Kagan
    Black walnut, ash splines and pegs
    h. 1.07 m
    USA, 1982

221 Plank-back chair
    Robert Williams
    Oak
    h. 90 cm
    UK, 1983

222 Mariabronn writing table
    Richard Kagan
    Black walnut, ash splines
    h. 72 cm
    USA, 1981

223 Table
    William Keyser
    Cherry, walnut
    h. 45 cm
    USA, 1978

Overleaf
224 Homage to Hoffmann
    Shiro Kuramata
    Steel rod, enamel finish
    h. 83 cm
    Japan, 1985

CHRONOLOGY

Few breakthroughs, however daring, are without roots. A characteristic of the modern age – from the late 18th century onwards – is the increase in the exchange of information. Emigration, travel, trade and international exhibitions (beginning with the Great Exhibition, London 1851) have been important conduits for ideas. So too have journals. Among the influential magazines existing in 1900 were *Art et Décoration*, Paris (1897) and *The Studio*, London (1893). As for exhibitions, the *Exposition Universelle*, Paris (1900), for example, brought Scandinavian design to international attention, whilst the Dresden Exhibition of Applied Art (1906) spurred the founding of the Deutsche Werkbund.

1900　Charles Rennie Mackintosh's high-backed chairs exhibited at the Vienna Secession. Mackintosh was influential in Europe, less so in Britain.
　　　Thonet Company: Michael Thonet began in Germany (1830), experimenting with laminated wood, moved to Austria and set up factory in 1849 producing bentwood chairs. In 1900 daily production of furniture reached a prodigious scale: writers John Fleming and Hugh Honour say 4,000 pieces a day, but Russell, Garner and Read claim 15,000. Authorities do agree that Thonet's most famous product, chair no. 14, is an early modern classic which was first produced in 1859 and was later favoured by Le Corbusier. Thonet had salerooms throughout Europe, in the US and also Russia. The company continues to flourish.

1903　Wiener Werkstätte founded in Vienna by Josef Hoffmann and Koloman Moser (designers) and Fritz Wärndorfer (banker). Inspired by Charles Ashbee's Guild of Handicraft (Britain, 1898–1907), it became a leading design organization, with regular exhibitions and a magazine. It ended in 1932.
　　　Frank Lloyd Wright (USA) produced his Oak chair for the Dana House, Springfield, Illinois. Wright followed this with severe, architectural furniture designs in 1904, 1908 and 1913 that anticipated the radicalism of the post-First World War European furniture designs (e.g., Gerrit Rietveid's Blue and Red chair). Fleming and Honour say his most important contribution to design was in 1904 when he produced angular, painted metal furniture for his Larkin Office building in Buffalo, New York. The first decade of the 20th century would have belonged to Wright, but his achievements were swamped by the dominance of European movements and the Bauhaus in the decade after the First World War.

1906　Otto Wagner's Post Office Savings Bank (with his furnishings) opened in Vienna. A key modern building, as important in its influence upon design as Charles Rennie Mackintosh's Glasgow Art School building and furnishings (1898).

1907　Deutsche Werkbund founded in Munich to promote German design. The first chairman was Theodor Fischer, architect. The Werkbund's aim was: 'The improvement of industrial products through the combined efforts of artists, craftsmen and industrialists.' It was influential and active: it published a year book (1912–20); it published a magazine

called *Die Form* (1925–34). In 1924 it organized a travelling exhibition, 'Form without Ornament'; in 1927 it constructed an exhibition of housing. It ceased in 1934 because of conflicts with the Nazis. The Werkbund appeared again in 1947, but its pioneering days were over.

1908　Adolf Loos, architect and writer, published *Ornament and Crime* and argued that fondness for ornament was a sign of undeveloped consciousness.

1914　Walter Gropius and Adolf Meyer's Fagus shoe factory opens in Germany: it represented an important stage in the development of the glass-wall concept, the signature of the international style in architecture.
　　　Henry Ford's Model T produced on a modern mass-manufacturing basis for the first time.
　　　Le Corbusier develops schemes for mass-produced housing.

1915　Design and Industries Association (UK) established. Modelled on the Deutsche Werkbund, it had its first exhibition at the Whitechapel Gallery.

1917　Red and Blue chair designed and made by Gerrit Rietveld. He was influenced by Frank Lloyd Wright and De Stijl, the latter founded in the same year.
　　　An exhibition of design in Stockholm stressed the importance of social awareness in industrial design.

1919　Bauhaus opened in Weimar, directed by Walter Gropius. Initially crafts orientated, but after the 1925 move to Dessau, an industrial design curriculum w　introduced. Gropius secured the services of: Paul Klee, Johannes Itten, Wassily Kandinsky, Moholy-Nagy, Adolf Meyer and Marcel Breuer. He resigned in 1928, and was replaced by Hannes Meyer and then in 1930 by Ludwig Mies van der Rohe. The Bauhaus moved to Berlin in 1932 and was dissolved by the Nazis in 1933. The New Bauhaus was re-formed in Chicago under Moholy-Nagy in 1935. It became the Chicago Institute of Design.

The period between the two World Wars was the high point of the modern movement in Europe, but although Breuer, Gropius, Mies van der Rohe and others espoused industrial techniques and mass production, it was largely the Americans who put ideas into production. For example, Chicago became a major centre for furniture trade. The American Furniture Mart there had expanded to 2 million square feet by 1926. The Chicago based Howell Company imported samples of Breuer's work, adapted it for production and by 1933 its range of tubular steel furniture included items for the home, office and showrooms.

1920　Cassina founded in Italy. After the Second World War it became famous for manufacturing designs by Mario Bellini, Vico Magistretti, Gaetano Pesce and many others.

1924　Eileen Gray, born in Ireland (1878), designed her Lota sofa in France. An important designer, her work was admired by relatively few people (including Le Corbusier) until 1968, when *domus* rediscovered her. Since the early 1970s Zeev

Aram, London, has brought many of her designs into manufacture, some for the first time.

1925 Marcel Breuer designed his Wassily chair at the Bauhaus: chromium nickel-plated steel frame and leather arms, seat, backrest – an exercise in describing volume with line and plane.
At the Arts Décoratifs et Industriels Modernes exhibition in Paris, the growing strength of Scandinavian design was confirmed. Among the important pieces shown was an armchair by Gunnar Asplund. It is currently in the Nordiska Museet, Stockholm.

1926 Mart Stam, Dutch architect and designer, developed designs for cantilevered chairs. These become much copied. Wharton Esherick, founder-father of the American woodcraft movement, begins building his extraordinary cubist-cum-Dr Caligari studio and house in Pennsylvania (completed 1966).

1928 Marcel Breuer's tubular steel cantilever chair. Le Corbusier designs *grand confort* armchair. Charlotte Perriand designed furniture and fittings for the Salon des Artistes Décorateurs. Le Corbusier and Perriand produce their chaise longue: symbol of the modern movement, of confidence in the future – and also of wealth.
domus design magazine founded in Italy by Gio Ponti.

1929 Union des Artistes Modernes founded in Paris, with first president Robert Mallet Stevens: a designer whose writings and furniture emphasized commitment to new materials and opposition to ornament.
Ludwig Mies van der Rohe launches the Barcelona chair: chrome-plated flat steel frame and fabric- or leather-covered horsehair cushions for seat and back.

1930 The Finnish architect Alvar Aalto began work on his famous Paimio chair in moulded plywood – final version 1933. Aalto's Paimio chair, his stacking chairs, his teacart of 1933 have all been influential, and his aesthetic is the one which dominated many welfare-state interiors in Scandinavia and in Britain.

1931 Practical Equipment Ltd (PEL) formed, bringing modern furniture to the UK. Its most famous product is the stacking chair in tubular metal and canvas – the RP6, a version of Mart Stam's 1926 chair, which is still exported all over the world.

1933 The first of the Milan Triennales – showplaces for Italian design.

1938 Knoll Associates founded in the US by Hans Knoll. Knoll married Florence Schust, who took over the company in 1955 when the founder died. Knoll Associates has subsidiary companies all over the world (Knoll International).

1939 US art critic Clement Greenberg publishes his seminal essay on 'Modernism, Avant Garde and Kitsch' in the *Partisan Review*.
During the Second World War many advances in materials technology were made with aluminium, plastics and plywood. The aircraft industry in particular led the way, not only in materials development, but in manufacturing processes generally, especially in the standardization of parts and machine-tool accuracy.

1943 Production of Utility furniture in Britain began under the direction of furniture designer Gordon Russell. This famous exercise in institutionalized good taste was a failure: as soon as rationing eased in the early 1950s, most people threw it out. Today designers revere it.

The decade and a half following the Second World War was dominated by Scandinavian design and the graduates of

Cranbrook Academy, Michigan. Commentators temper the view that Scandinavia dominated through excellence alone, pointing out that Scandinavian influence waned once Italy and West Germany had built their economies. Graduates of Cranbrook who came to prominence in the 1940s and 1950s include Charles and Ray Eames, Eero Saarinen, Harry Bertoia and Florence Schust Knoll.

1946 Ernest Race's BA Chair launched in Britain.

1946 Le Corbusier's Unité d'Habitation in Marseilles begun (completed 1952). The design is based on Le Corbusier's modular system of harmonic proportions taken from the human figure. Charles Eames's Eames chair, with moulded plywood and steel frame, launched by Herman Miller in the US. Womb chair designed by Eero Saarinen. Manufactured by Knoll 1948.

1948 Charles Eames worked on his design for a moulded fibreglass armchair (completed 1950).

1949 Kartell started in Italy. It became the first company to mould nylon products and manufacture seats entirely in plastic.

1951 Ernest Race's Antelope chair launched in the UK. Arne Jacobsen's stacking chair launched in Denmark by Fritz Hansen.
Milan Triennales resume.

1952 Harry Bertoia's steel lattice Diamond chairs were first produced for Knoll in the US.

1954 A major exhibition, 'Design in Scandinavia', toured America and Canada until 1957.
Aurelia Zanotta (Italy) founds the Zanotta Company.

1955 Ulm University of Industrial Design opened in the spirit of the Bauhaus. One of Ulm's graduates is Ferdinand Alexander Porsche, designer of the 84 S recliner.

1956 Charles Eames lounge chair and ottoman launched by Herman Miller. Pedestal chair by Eero Saarinen manufactured by Knoll International.

1957 Achille Castiglioni's seminal Mezzadro (tractor) seat launched by Zanotta. Sputnik launched by USSR, world's first venture into space.

Changes occurred in the 1960s which have determined the fate of contemporary design: the West European economies became stronger (apart from that of the UK); technological change quickened, spurred by consumer booms and the defence industries; the travel industry expanded, as did the exchange of ideas and imagery via magazines, television, and people studying or teaching abroad. Pluralism and the concept of fashion entered design. The 1960s generated new imagery and in this Britain and the USA – through their pop art movements – provided a source of ideas (and kitsch) which has fed Italian design well into the 1980s. By the end of the 1960s a craft revival was under way; this dominated furniture design in Britain and the USA and endorsed the soft modernism, wood-orientated approach of the Scandinavians.

1961 Annual Milan furniture fairs started.

1964 Robin Day's polypropylene chair launched with Hille (UK). David Rowland's classic stacking chair, the G40 – manufactured by General Fireproofing, USA. Marco Zanuso's (Italy) and Richard Sapper's (West Germany) child's chair in polythene for Kartell.
Terence Conran (UK) opens the first of the chain of Habitat stores which offered the modern look at cheap prices – a

marketing strategy that had long worked well in Scandinavia.

1966 Archizoom Associati founded in Italy by Andrea Branzi, Gilberto Corretti, Paolo Deganello and Massimo Morozzi. It specialized in architecture and urban research and one of its famous projects is No-stop City (see *The Hot House* by Andrea Branzi). Its records are preserved at the Archives of Communication of the Institute for the History of Art at the University of Parma.
Superstudio was established. Another radical Italian design group.
First version of the Ergon office chair by Bill Stumpf for Herman Miller.
Complexity and Contradiction in Architecture by Robert Venturi published. It began the debate about reviving ornament.

1967 Blow – the inflatable armchair manufactured by Zanotta.

1968 Driade founded.
Launch of the Action Office walled office system designed by Bill Stumpf for Herman Miller. This was the definitive office system for a decade. The new Ethospace system seeks a similar role into the 1990s.

1969 Plia folding chairs – aluminium and clear plastic designed by Giancarlo Piretti for Castelli in Italy. The Sacco chair (a pear-shaped leather sack filled with polystyrene pellets and then sealed) launched by Zanotta. Designed by Gatti, Paolini, Teodoro.
First man (American) on the moon.

1970 End, according to Reyner Banham, critic, of the modern movement.

1971 Crafts Advisory Committee (later the Crafts Council) started in London.

1972 'Italy: The New Domestic Landscape' at the Museum of Modern Art, New York.

1975 Charles Jencks, architect and critic, begins writing about post-modernism.

1976 Alchymia (Alessandro Mendini among its members) launched. It showed important collections of furniture in 1978, 1979, 1980.

1977 Pompidou Centre, Paris, opened. Designed by Richard Rogers and Renzo Piano.

John Makepeace established his school for craftsmen in wood at Parnham House, UK.

1978 Philip Johnson's AT&T building begun in New York. Critic Deyan Sudjic comments: 'it marked the acceptance of post modernism in America's corporate style.' Alessandro Mendini designed the Proust chair. Like many of the later 1970s and early 1980s designs (such as those produced by Memphis) Proust's role was polemical, whereas Mendini's Club chair in the San Leonardo collection (1985) is for use.

1980 Balans Duo developed for Westnofa (Norway) by Peter Opsvik. Work began on Michael Graves' post-modern City Office building, Portland, Ohio. Toshiyuk Kita designs Wink for Cassina, Italy.

1981 The Memphis group began, with Renzo Brigola, Mario and Brunella Godani, Fausto Celati and Ernesto Gismondi. It has produced designs by Ettore Sottsass, Andrea Branzi and Matteo Thun. The art director is Barbara Radice. Casablanca sideboard by Ettore Sottsass shown for the first time: it became the archetypal Memphis image. Journalist Tom Wolfe published his attack on modernism in an extended essay in *Harper's – From Bauhaus to Our House* – subsequently published as a book.

1982 All-plastic table for Kartell by Anna Castelli Ferrieri. Domus Academy offering postgraduate courses in the new design, started in Milan.

1984 Robert Venturi's bentwood post-modern chairs launched by Knoll International.
The Hot House: Italian New Wave Design by Andrea Branzi published: part history, part futurology and part manifesto.

1985 4873 all-plastic armchair made by Kartell and designed by Anna Castelli Ferrieri.

1986 Foster Associates' headquarters for Hong Kong and Shanghai Bank opened in Hong Kong. Richard Rogers' Lloyds Building, London opened. Nomos (UK/Italy), Ethospace (USA) and From Nine to Five (Italy) office systems launched. Each sets new standards for quality of working environment. The new sobriety in the Milan salon is demonstrated by Ettore Sottsass's new chairs Bridge and Mandarin for Knoll International.

1987 Driade launch new range of Philippe Starck's furniture at the Cologne Furniture Fair.

BIOGRAPHIES

Notes on a number of the figures who are shaping contemporary trends in furniture design.

Arad, Ron b.Israel 1951. Studied architecture at the Architectural Association, London. He founded the One-Off design company and gallery in London in 1981; this is now a focal point of alternative furniture design in Britain. Arad's Rover car-seat armchair (1983) has become a classic demonstration of recycling existing design. His Hi-fi system set in concrete caused much debate among more orthodox product designers. Arad's alertness to the variety of texture possible in metal is stimulating a greater awareness generally of the decorative nuances that can be achieved with industrial materials. And although the imagery of his furniture is industrial, it is not high-tech; in some respects it is a nostalgic resurrection of industrial craft.

Astori, Antonia b.Italy 1940. Studied industrial and visual design at Lausanne University, graduating in 1966. She began her collaboration with the Italian furniture manufacturing company Driade in 1968. Her particular specialism is systems furniture, which she has helped to pioneer: her first system design was Driade 1 (1968), followed by Oikos (1972). In 1977 she worked with Enzo Mari to produce Bric, and in 1980 designed Oikos-due. Her most recent work includes a range of furniture called Aforisme. See the book by B. Gravagnuolo, *Antonia Astori*, 1983. She was a Compasso d'Oro prize winner in 1981 for her work in creating the Driade Company image. The Driade Company itself manufactures Astori's work to a high standard. Although the units are self-assembly (coated chipboard and flat-packed units), the quality of finish is much higher than run of the mill knock-down furniture. Indeed, the final paint surfaces are applied by hand.

Atkinson, Paul b.UK 1952. Studied design at Leicester Polytechnic and the Royal College of Art, London. He is a partner of Atkinson Design Associates and his designs include lighting for Rotaflex (UK), electrical products and furniture. He has done project work for Knoll International and his designs in production include the widely acclaimed PA chair for Hille Ergonom (1985).

Bakker, Gijs b.Holland 1942. Studied gold and silversmithing at the Amsterdam Art Academy. Well known as a radical jeweler and sculptor, he has been producing furniture designs since 1972 and has also produced a number of product designs. His chairs include the Strip chair (1974) and the Finger chair (1979). Bakker argues: 'In my opinion, the designer should be someone who is outside the firm for which he works, who learns to understand it, but who remains detached. He should be well informed on cultural and social matters, and bring this knowledge with him into the firm.'

Ball, Douglas b.Canada 1935. Studied industrial design at the Ontario College of Arts, Toronto. He has won several Canadian design awards and is well known for his Race office system for Sunar Hauserman. His other commissions include transportation and public seating systems, and also wheelchair designs for physically disabled users.

Bellini, Mario b.Italy 1935. Studied architecture at the Milan Polytechnic, graduating in 1959. He runs an architectural and design practice in Milan. He is well known as a teacher and as an editor of the magazine *domus*. He has worked with Artemide, Erco, Fiat, B&B Italia, Poltrona Frau, Marcatre and Cassina, and is now head of office machine design for Olivetti. Among his famous furniture designs is the Cab chair for Cassina (1977). He has won the Compasso d'Oro many times and other design prizes in Spain, West Germany and the USA.

Branzi, Andrea b.Italy. Studied architecture in Florence. Works as a writer and designer. A leading intellectual in Italian design, he was a founder member of Archizoom Associati in 1966. In 1979 he won the Compasso d'Oro for his research into primary design; his lectures have been published under the title *Goods and the Metropolis* (1984). He is educational director of the Domus Academy and his best-known book to date is *The Hot House: Italian New Wave Design* (1984). The latter is in part a manifesto. For him design is a practical philosophical enterprise embracing both semantics and architecture (and much in between). He is opposed to grand designs, and he is concerned with reclaiming the modern city from the sphere of public bureaucracy and anonymity, and pulling it into the domestic realm or the psychological space of the ordinary individual. He ends *The Hot House* with a quotation: 'Let's leave big systems to little improvisers.'

Burns, Mark b.USA 1950. Studied fine art at the University of Washington, Seattle, and graduated with a Masters degree in 1974. Although his main medium is clay, he is used to creating mixed media objects and installations. He casts an oblique mind over contemporary domestic objects. His imagination is helped by his wide knowledge of, and deep interest in, the urban vernacular of American consumerism. He has exhibited widely in the USA. See the catalogue *Contemporary Arts: An Expanding View* (Helen Drutt Gallery, Philadelphia, 1986).

Carter, Ronald b.UK 1926. Studied interior design at Birmingham College of Art, followed by furniture design at the Royal College of Art, London. He was awarded the title of Royal Designer for Industry in 1974. In 1980 he and the manufacturer Peter Miles formed the Carter/Miles Company. The company produces a wide range of Carter's designs, many of which – such as the Whitney dining chairs (1981) – have become acknowledged as classics. Carter and Miles have completed many corporate commissions. Clients include the British Broadcasting Corporation and the British Airports Authority. Carter's work is rooted in both Tudor and Shaker imagery and his style is spare, but the proportions (such as the width and depth of a seat) are generous.

Castle, Wendell b.USA 1932. Studied sculpture at the University of Kansas and graduated with a Masters degree in 1961. Castle is the

USA's best-known independent furniture producer. In the 1960s he pioneered an approach to laminating stacks of wood and then carving it into organic forms for use as chairs or settees. He then produced a range of *trompe l'oeil* pieces of sculptural-furniture, 'Still Lives'. These wood sculptures, of dazzling technical dexterity, have been followed by grand pieces of furniture that are elaborately worked in expensive materials. Castle explains: 'I'm continuing the furniture tradition using the same decorative vocabulary that's been around for 400 years but keeping in step with the times.' His work sells for tens of thousands of dollars.

Castiglioni, Achille b.Italy 1918. Studied architecture in Milan and graduated in 1944. He set up a design studio with his two brothers Livio and Pier Giacomo. Castiglioni has been a prolific prize winner (Compasso d'Oro won seven times) and he is the Professor of Interior Architecture at the Turin Polytechnic. He has many notable designs to his credit, including Mezzadro – a little tractor-seat stool designed in 1955; Primate – a stool to kneel into (1970); and a conference table/desk for Marcatre (1982). He has several designs in the permanent collection at the Museum of Modern Art, New York. Castiglioni is respected because his designs work and they are inventive. He is, however, sceptical about the way that design has become fashion- rather than ideas-orientated. In his view, new designs have to be justified by a need that is more than a simple desire for stylistic change.

Crutch, Peter b.UK 1940. Studied design at Leicester College of Art and the Royal College of Art, London. Worked with the architect Sir Basil Spence and then in the offices of Sir Terence Conran. He joined Fitch and Co. in 1970 and was responsible for the Gull Wing terminus seating first used in terminal 4 of London Heathrow Airport (opened 1986). Gull Wing has brought fresh imagery to fixed seating without compromising practicality or indulging in historicist whimsy. Its special aspect is in its knock-down construction: thus it can be transported economically and damaged parts can be replaced without replacing the whole unit.

Deganello, Paolo b.Italy 1940. Studied architecture at the University of Florence. A founder member of the Archizoom design group, he is well known as a teacher and theorist. He has designed for a number of companies, including Cassina and Marcatre.

Diffrient, Niels b.USA 1928. He studied at Cranbrook Academy, Michigan, with fellow students such as Florence Knoll and Charles Eames. Diffrient is an expert on ergonomics and some designers consider his Helena office chair to be 'definitive'. Most recently, his Jefferson executive chair-as-office (from which one can almost run the world) is attracting much interest. Among his major clients are Sunar Hauserman, Honeywell, Lockheed, Hughes Aircraft and Knoll International. He is co-author (with Alvin R. Tilley) of *Humanscale 1–2–3* (Cambridge, Massachusetts, 1974), and *Humanscale 4–5–6* and *Humanscale 7–8–9* (both 1981).

Ferrieri, Anna Castelli b.Italy 1920. Studied architecture at the Milan Polytechnic, graduating in 1942. She is an urban planner, as well as an architect and industrial designer. Her first major award was a gold medal for modular kitchen units shown at the Milan Triennale in 1951. She has done a number of major designs for Kartell, including modular furniture and kitchen and tableware, which received a Compasso d'Oro in 1979. Her industrial design has recently included a solar-assisted town car. She is one of the few furniture designers on the world stage who has kept alive the concept of serving people's needs regardless of their class or status.

She rebuffs those designers who argue that mass production is necessarily only useful for serving average needs: a good design is a good design and should suit human beings *qua* human beings.

Foster, Norman b.UK 1935. Studied architecture at the University of Manchester and at Yale. Established Foster Associates in 1967. Foster is one of the world's leading architects; his buildings include the headquarters of Willis Faber and Dumas at Ipswich and the headquarters for the Hong Kong and Shanghai Bank. Foster's work is represented in the Museum of Modern Art, New York. His office furniture system Nomos was launched by its manufacturer, Tecno, in Milan in 1986. Despite criticisms, the Nomos range is already regarded as an important contribution to office planning.

Graves, Michael b.USA 1934. Studied architecture at Harvard University. He is now the best-known post-modernist architect, and he came to international fame with his Public Services Building in Oregon (1982) and Humana Building in Louisville, Kentucky (1985). He has designed furniture for the Memphis group and Sunar Hauserman – he did the interior of Sunar's London showrooms in 1986.

Gusrud, Svein b.Norway 1944. Studied design at the Oslo National School of Art and Design. He is highly inventive and has a sense of humour which helps him find new solutions to old problems – especially that of coping with people who want to sit, rest or wait comfortably in the numerous public spaces of modern life. So far it seems that his 'leaners' have only attracted a curiosity value.

Hakala, Pentti b.Finland 1949. Studied art history and philosophy at Jyvaskyla University (1969–73), then design at the University of Industrial Arts (1977–83). His work has been taken up by the Finnish Design Council and his prize-winning chairs have marked him out as as important new design talent in Scandinavia.

Iavicoli, Vincenzo b.Italy 1957. Studied industrial design at the State Institute of Industrial Design in Florence. Since 1980 he has worked with Maria Luisa Rossi. Their work is radical and an inventive crossing of all the borders of design, craft and art.

Kinsman, Rodney b.UK 1943. Studied furniture design at the Central School of Art, London. In 1966 he began OMK – first a design consultancy, later a manufacturing company. Kinsman's work includes the highly successful Graffiti shelving and storage system; furniture launched in the 1980s includes the Vienna and Tokyo ranges. His preferred materials are steel, glass, rubber and vinyl. Kinsman is the longest established of the independent British designer-manufacturers, and throughout the 1970s he was more or less on his own in Britain. His work is also made under licence by Bieffeplast in Italy.

Kuramata, Shiro b.Japan 1934. Trained in architecture and later in cabinet-making. He is an interior designer as well as a furniture designer, and has designed shops for the internationally known fashion designer Issey Miyake. His most famous single furniture pieces are his glass chair (1976) and Homage to Hoffmann, Begin the Bigin (1985). Kuramata is one of those designers who (like Arad, Morrison and Thun, for example) are particularly alert to nuances in 'industrialized' or non-natural surfaces. He has rescued the non-natural surface from blandness. See the catalogue *The Works of Shiro Kuramata 1967–1981* (Parco, ISBN 4–89194–059 X).

Magistretti, Vico b.Italy 1920. Graduated in architecture from Milan University in 1945 and went to work in his father's practice. In the

1960s he began designing furniture and since then he has worked with a number of manufacturers, including Knoll International and Cassina. Some of his work is in the permanent design collection of the Museum of Modern Art, New York. Among Magistretti's notable designs are the Selene all-plastic chair, manufactured by Artemide in 1968, the Maralunga sofa (Cassina, 1973), and the Villabianca chairs (Cassina, 1985). He won the Compasso d'Oro in 1967 and 1979, the gold medal at the 9th Milan Triennale and the first prize of the International Jury at the Cologne Furniture Fair in 1982. Some of his most recent work (the 1986 Cardigan sofa, for example) has been criticised as dull. Others see it as simply quiet, a measured attempt to serve the domestic landscape rather than bawling egocentrically in it.

Makepeace, John b.UK 1939. He has had no formal training as a designer but has had considerable influence on British craft furniture with his school for craftsmen in wood (established 1977). Opinion as to the merits of his own design work is sharply divided, opinion about his craftsmanship is generally not – he is regarded as one of the best makers of furniture in Britain.

Mari, Enzo b.Italy 1932. Studied at the Brera Academy of Fine Art in Milan. He has designed children's games, books, glass and furniture. Mari has worked with Driade, for whom he designed the Delfina chair which won the Compasso d'Oro award in 1979. Other important designs include the Sof Sof chair (1971) and Frate tables (1974).

Mendini, Alessandro b.Italy 1931. Designer and writer. He worked for Nizzoli Associates (a leading Italian industrial design group) until 1970. He was a founder member of global tools – a school of counter-architecture and design established in 1973. He has collaborated with Alessi, Cassina and others, and won a Compasso d'Oro award for design in 1979. Publications include *Good-bye Architecture* (1981) and *The Unhappy Project* (1983). He directed *Casabella*, the architectural magazine (1970–76), and the fashion editions of *domus* (1976–85).

Morozzi, Massimo b.Italy 1941. Studied architecture and was a member of Archizoom Associati. From 1972 to 1977 he ran the Montefibre Design Centre, which developed furnishing and textile products. As a consequence, he has worked with Driade on the Driadesoft range of furniture. His own studio, Massimo Morozzi Design, opened in 1982.

Morrison, Jasper b.UK 1959. Studied design at Kingston Polytechnic and the Royal College of Art, London. His work displays truth to materials, appropriate technology and search for harmony in proportion: the virtues of modernism and, ironically, the crafts movement – ironic since Morrison deplores the contemporary crafts scene as self-indulgent.

Nurmesniemi, Antti b.Finland 1927. Studied interior design at the Institute of Industrial Arts in Helsinki, graduating in 1950. He has designed interiors for a wide range of buildings and furniture for Artek, Lifjaama and Merivaara. He is an early example of the wide-ranging industrial designer – his Finel coffee pot of 1958 has become ubiquitous in Finland; his glassware, wallpaper and textiles are successful; and he has also done transportation design for the Helsinki Metro.

Opsvik, Peter b.Norway 1939. Graduated in design in 1964. He worked as an industrial designer for the Tandberg Radio company (1965–70). He has worked as a freelance industrial designer since 1972. Perhaps his most famous design is the Balans variable seat (1980).

Peters, Alan b.UK 1933. Apprenticed to Edward Barnsley, son of Sidney Barnsley, one of the major figures of the British arts and crafts movement. Studied at Shoreditch College, London, and then interior design at the Central School of Arts and Crafts, London. Established his own craft workshop in 1962. His work shows some influence from trips made to Japan, Korea and Taiwan. Peters is one of the leading craftsmen in Britain and he has work in the Victoria and Albert Museum, London.

Porsche, Ferdinand Alexander b.West Germany 1935. He studied at the Ulm University of Design. After work in an electrical company he joined the family car business and until 1972 was responsible for styling. His designs include the Porsche 904 and 911 sports cars. In 1972 he established a separate design studio in Stuttgart, and then in 1974 he set up Porsche Design in Zell-am-Zee in Austria. All Porsche designs are engineered in high-quality materials. Whether it is furniture, briefcases, sunglasses or wrist watches, Porsche designs manage to become cult objects; they are a contemporary proof of the late 20th-century desire to make fashionableness of design an end in itself.

Rossi, Maria Luisa b.Italy 1958. Graduated from the Institute of Industrial Design in Florence and attended the Domus Academy from which she graduated in 1984. She has worked in Studio Alchymia. She and Vincenzo Iavicoli are founder members of the Salotto Dinamico Studio.

Sapper, Richard b.West Germany 1932. Studied philosophy, anatomy, graphics, engineering, and graduated in business economics from the University of Munich. Joined Mercedes Benz. Left in 1958 to work with Gio Ponti in Italy. Consultancy work followed for Fiat, Pirelli and, since 1980, IBM (where he is head of product design). He has won the Compasso d'Oro five times. His work is in the Museum of Modern Art, New York. His famous designs include the award-winning Tizio lamp, a genuine classic, and a kettle for Alessi which, for utilitarian reasons, some people have found less convincing. His From Nine to Five office furniture for Castelli, launched at the end of 1986, is highly regarded.

Scott, Fred b.UK 1942. Worked as an apprentice cabinet-maker in High Wycombe and then studied design at the Royal College of Art, London. He joined Hille International (UK – now Hille Ergonom) in 1969 as a freelance designer. His Supporto office chair (1979) has been a considerable aesthetic, practical and commercial success for the company.

Sottsass, Ettore b.Austria 1917, Italian citizen. Studied architecture at the Turin Polytechnic, graduating in 1939. Sottsass is an industrial designer, furniture designer and artist – he has produced paintings, illustrations, sculptures, and also designed in metal and for ceramics. He was associated in the 1960s with 'anti-design' and his Memphis group in the 1980s produced a rupture in orthodox design thinking – in particular, it showed other designers the importance of the decorative surface, and also alerted them to the importance of texture (both implied, i.e. visual) and actual. His work for Olivetti is famous, especially the Valentine typewriter and the Synthesis office chair, a brightly coloured adjustable typist's seat which looks functional and toy-like at the same time. Both products emerged in 1969. He has won the Compasso d'Oro several times and in 1980 he formed a design firm – Sottsass Associati. This has grown rapidly as an architectural as well as a design studio, and it has also spawned an American offshoot called Enorme, an electronics design company.

Starck, Philippe b.France 1949. Began his professional career as a designer working with Pierre Cardin. Came to fame with his furniture designs for President Mitterand's Elysée Palace apartment. He is a prolific designer, who has worked for Renault, as well as designing a cigarette lighter, television sets and wrist watches. His role as an international figure is analogous to that of a world pop star. Among the companies with whom he has had a close manufacturing relationship is Driade. His furniture is indisputably gracious and conveys luxury without ornamentalist excess.

Stumpf, Bill b.USA 1936. Graduated in industrial design at the University of Illinois and in environmental design at the University of Wisconsin. Stumpf was research director (design) and a vice-president of Herman Miller from 1970 to 1973. He subsequently formed a design partnership with Donald Chadwick (Chadwick, Stumpf and Associates). Stumpf was voted as designer of the 1970s by the American Industrial Design magazine. He has won many awards and his famous designs include the Ergon chair (first version 1966) and the Ethospace office system (1985). The Chadwick-Stumpf partnership is a fruitful one: they avoid recondite philosophy, but have introduced into office design a mixture of practical engineering (Chadwick: 'Remember the old meat grinder your grandmother had? Anybody could take it apart and figure out how it went back together. There was a logic to its construction') and the humane. In Ethospace the possibilities exist for making the office almost domestic and in the Equa chair (developed 1979–84) the imagery is organic. It is a philosophy of being modern and scientific and homespun. And people like it.

Thun, Matteo b.Austria 1952. Studied architecture at the University of Florence. He was a founder-member of the Memphis group. He runs his own architectural and design practice in Milan and he is Professor of Product Design at the School of Applied Arts in Vienna. Thun has coined the expression 'the Baroque Bauhaus' – it describes the thinking in the philosophical area that lies between the Ulm University of Industrial Design and the Memphis-led Milan salon of urban 20th-century Baroque. Thun is searching for images that will succeed in 'communicating the sense of wellbeing' that he believes can be bred out of the Milan-versus-Ulm scuffles.

Van den Broecke, Floris b.Holland 1945. Studied painting at Arnhem Academy and furniture design at the Royal College of Art, London. He is both a designer and a maker of furniture, although designing has taken precedence since the formation in 1985 of his partnership, Furniture Designers, with Peter Wheeler and Jane Dillon. Van den Broecke is Professor of Furniture Design at the Royal College of Art, London.

Venturi, Robert b.USA 1925. Studied architecture at the University of Princeton. He is a partner in the architectural practice Venturi, Rauch and Scott Brown, and is one of the pioneers of post-modernist architecture. His seminal books on post-modernism are *Complexity and Contradiction in Modern Architecture* (1966) and *Learning from Las Vegas* (1972). His range of furniture for Knoll International was launched in 1984. Venturi declared his philosophy on furniture some years before: 'A characteristic of orthodox Modern furniture has been its seriousness – its beauty deriving from severity rather than wit, elegance rather than sentiment, consistency rather than richness. And ornament, of course, has been taboo. What I propose is chairs, tables and bureaus that adapt a series of historical styles involving wit, variety, and industrial process, and consisting of a flat profile in a decorative shape in a frontal dimension.'

DESIGN-LED COMPANIES

A selection of commercial showrooms where good furniture design can be seen and bought. The addresses of the main office/showrooms are given, but some companies have offices throughout the world.

Aleph, Via Felice Casati 20, 20124 Milan, Italy
Aram Designs Ltd, 3 Kean Street, London, WC2 4AT, UK
Artifort, St Annalaan 23, 6214 AA Maastricht, Holland
Ateria, 6–3–11 802 Minami-Aoyama, Minato-ku, Tokyo 107, Japan
Authentics, 42 Shelton Street, London WC2H 9HZ
Baleri Italia, 24035 Curno, Bergamo, Italy
BD Mueblas, Mallorca 293, Barcelona, Spain
Bianchi, Via Como 15, 22060 Figino Serenza (10), Italy
Bieffeplast, PO Box 406, 1–35100 Padua, Italy
Casas, Milagro 40, 08028 Barcelona, Spain
Cassina SPA, 1 Via Busnelli, 20036 Meda, Milan, Italy
Castelijn Collection BV, Vrouwenweg LC, 3864 DX N Nijkerkerveen, Holland
Designers' Guild, 277 King's Road, London SW3 5EN, UK
Design, M, Ingo Maurer GMBH, Kaiserstrasse 47, 8000 Munich 40, West Germany
Disform, Ronda, General Mitre 63, 08017 Barcelona, Spain
Driade, Padana Inferiore, 29012 Caorso, Italy
Fritz Hansen Depotvej 1, DK–3450 Allerod, Denmark
Gordon Russell, Broadway, Worcestershire WR12 7AD, UK
Herman Miller, 8500 Byron Road, Zeeland, MI 49464, USA
Hille Ergonom, 356 Euston Road, London NW1, UK
Independent Designers' Federation, 30 Bruges Place, Randolph Street, London NW1
Inno Tuote oy, Merikatu 1, 00140 Helsinki 14, Finland

InterProfil, Karl Theodor-Strasse 91, D–8000 Munich 40, West Germany
Kartell, 1 Via delle Industrie, 20082 Noviglio (Mi), Italy
Knoll International, The Knoll Building, 655 Madison Avenue, New York, NY 10021, USA
Lammhults Mekaniska AB, PO Box 26, 36030 Lammhult, Sweden
Liberty and Co, Regent Street, London W1, UK
Magnus Olesen, 10 Tonderingvej-Durup, DK–7870 Roslev, Denmark
Marcatre, Via Sant'Andrea 3, 1–20020 Misinto, Milan, Italy
Memphis SRL, Via Breda 1, 20010 Pregnana, Milan, Italy
OMK Design, Stephen Building, Stephen Street, London W1P 1BN, UK
One-Off, 56 Neal Street, London WC2, UK
Poltrona Frau, 62029 Tolentino, Italy
Porsche Design, Flugplatzstrasse 29, A–5700 Zell-am-Zee, Austria
Proforma Hietalahdenkatu 4, 00180 Helsinki, Finland
Sheridan Coakely, 135–139 Curtain Road, London, EC2A 3BX, UK
Sunar Hauserman, 5711 Grant Avenue, Cleveland, OH 44105, USA
Tecno, Via Monte Napoleone 27c, Milan, Italy
Tecta Möbel, Sohnreystr, 4471 Lauenförde, West Germany
Thonet (Vienna), 11 A Untere Weissgerberstrasse, A–1030 Vienna, Austria
Thonet (West Germany), Michael Thonet Strasse, 3558 Frankenberg, West Germany (separate company from above)
Tribu, 88 Avenue Klèbes, 75116 Paris, France
Vitra, 59 Avenue d'Iena, 75116 Paris, France
Vuokko, Elimaenkatu 14–16, 00510 Helsinki, Finland
Zanotta Spa, Via Vittorio Veneto 57, 20054 Nova Milanese, Italy
Zeus, 8 Via Vigevano, 20144 Milan, Italy

GALLERIES AND MUSEUMS

These are a selection of the Galleries and Museums which either have collections of contemporary furniture or exhibit furniture.

USA

American Art Inc, 56 E. Andrews Drive N.W., Andrew Square, Atlanta, GA 30305

American Craft Museum, West 53rd Street, New York, NY 10019

Art et Industrie, 464 West Broadway, New York, NY 10012

Art Institute of Chicago, Michigan Avenue at Adams Street, Chicago, IL 60603

Cincinnati Contemporary Arts Centre, 115 E. 5th Street, Cincinnati, OH 45203

Cooper-Hewitt Museum, The Smithsonian Institution's National Museum of Design, 2 East 91st Street, New York

Gallery of the Applied Arts, 24 West 57th Street, New York, NY 10019

Global Furniture, 525 Broadway, New York, NY 10012

Helen Drutt Gallery, 1721 Walnut Street, Philadelphia, PA 19103

Indianapolis Museum of Art, 1200 W. 38 Street, Indianapolis, IN 46208

La Jolla Museum of Contemporary Art, La Jolla, California 92037

MIT Museum, 265 Massachusetts Avenue, Cambridge, MA

Mobili Decorative Arts, 1812 Adamsmill Road, Washington, D.C.

Museum of Modern Art, 11 West 53rd Street, New York, NY 10019

New York Design Centre, Thompson Avenue, Long Island City, New York, NY 11101

Philadelphia Museum of Art, Philadelphia, PA

Renwick Gallery of the National Museum of American Art (Smithsonian Institution), Pennsylvania Avenue at 17th Street, N.W., Washington, D.C. 20560

Signature: A Gallery of Furnishings, 55 Pacific Avenue, San Francisco, CA 94133

Snyderman Gallery, 317 South Street, Philadelphia, PA 19417

Whitney Museum of American Art, 75th Street and Madison Avenue, New York, NY 10021

Workbench, 470 Park Avenue South at 32nd Street, New York

Europe

Bauhaus Collections, Ernst Ludwig Haus, Mathildenhoe, 6100 Darmstadt, Hesse

Boymans-Van Beuningen Museum, Mathenesserlaan 18–20, Rotterdam, Holland

Crafts Council Gallery, Waterloo Place, London SW1, UK

Design Council, 28 Haymarket, London SW1, UK

Deutsches Architekturmuseum, Schaumainkai 43, Frankfurt-am-Main, West Germany

Helsinki Municipal Museum, Karamsininkatu 2, Helsinki 10, Finland

Kölnisches Stadtmuseum, Cologne, West Germany

Kunstindustrimuseet, Oslo, Norway

Kunstindustrimuset, 68 Bredgade, FK 1260 Copenhagen, Denmark

Kunstmuseum, Ehrenhof 3–5, Düsseldorf, West Germany

Le Corbusier, Heidi Weber House, Bellerivestrasse and Hoschgasse 8, Zurich, Switzerland

Musée des Arts Décoratifs, 107 rue de Rivoli, 75001 Paris, France

Museum für Gestaltung, Ausstellungstrasse 60, Zurich, Switzerland

Neotu, 25 rue du Renard, 75004 Paris, France

The New Collection, 22 Prinzregentenstrasse 3, 8000 Munich, West Germany

Nordenfjeldske Kunstidustrimuseum, Trondheim, Norway

Rohss Museum of Arts and Crafts, 37–9 Vasagatan, Gothenburg, Sweden

Sainsbury Centre, University of East Anglia, Norwich, Norfolk

Stedelijk Museum, Paulus Porterstraat 13, 5082 Amsterdam, Holland

Vestlandske Kunstindustrimuseum, Bergen, Norway

Victoria and Albert Museum, Cromwell Road SW7, London, UK

Villa La Roche (Le Corbusier Foundation), 10 Square Docteur Blanche, Paris 75016, France

EXHIBITIONS

A list of important exhibitions with catalogues

Each year there are several international furniture trade fairs: the most important are the Milan Furniture Fair (each September); the Cologne Furniture Fair (each January); the summer Scandinavian Furniture Fair, Copenhagen; and the office furnishings fair in Chicago (June)

1970   *Modern Chairs 1918–1970*, Whitechapel Gallery (arranged by the Victoria and Albert Museum, London)

1972   *Italy: The New Domestic Landscape*, Museum of Modern Art, New York. Curated by Emilio Ambasz, this exhibition confirmed Italy's design leadership. American critic Martin Filler wrote: ' "The New Domestic Landscape" showed clearly where some of the most widely copied designs of the sixties and early seventies came from.' It showed Italian design as a philosophical, speculative and subversive enterprise

1973   *Charles Eames: Furniture From the Design Collection*, The Museum of Modern Art, New York

1974   *Utility Furniture and Fashion*, Geffrye Museum, London

1975   *Change of Pace: Contemporary Furniture 1925–1975*, Cincinnati Art Museum, Cincinnati, Ohio

1975   *Der Deutscher Werkbund*, Staatliches Museum für Angewandte Kunst, Munich

1976   *The Design of Herman Miller*, Whitney Museum of American Art, New York. An important summation of the work done by the company which, together with Knoll International, has led practical design innovation in the USA

1977   *Ludwig Mies van der Rohe: Furniture and Furniture Drawings from the Design Collection*, Museum of Modern Art, New York. This was the definitive exhibition of Mies van der Rohe's furniture. The catalogue is slim, but very good

1977   *Practical Equipment Limited*, Architectural Association, London. This exhibition's well-written catalogue, illustrated with pre-Second World War pictures and reproducing information from the company's brochures, provides an excellent demonstration of how a design-led manufacturing company is the essential conduit between design philosophy and our everyday world

1977   *The Modern Chair: Its Origins and Evolution*, La Jolla Museum of Contemporary Art, La Jolla, California

1979   *Eileen Gray: Designer 1879–1976*, Victoria and Albert Museum, London, and Museum of Modern Art, New York

1980   *Métiers de l'Art*, Musée des Arts Décoratifs, Paris

1980   *Mobel italienisches Design: Kultur und Technologie im italienischen*, Kölnisches Stadtmuseum, Cologne, West Germany

1981   *Innovative Furniture in America*, Cooper-Hewitt, New York

1982   *Italian Re Evolution: Design in Italian Society in the Eighties*, La Jolla Museum of Contemporary Art, La Jolla, California

1982   *Shape and Environment: Furniture by American Architects*, Whitney Museum of American Art, New York

1983   *Design Since 1945*, Philadelphia Museum of Art, Philadelphia,

Pennsylvania. An exhibition of considerable importance; the catalogue – published as a book in the UK under the same title – is a work of reference which is essential for anyone interested in furniture design and design generally

1983   *Design in America: The Cranbrook Vision 1925 to 1950*, Metropolitan Museum of Art, New York. Cranbrook is as important to design in the USA as the Bauhaus/Ulm University are to Europe

1983   *Scandinavian Modern Design: 1880–1980*, Cooper-Hewitt Museum, New York. A major exhibition with an excellent catalogue (see books)

1983   *Taste*, Conran Foundation, Victoria and Albert Museum, London. This exhibition was roundly condemned by most critics, but it was popular and stimulating: it sought to define good and bad taste, and pondered the nature of Kitsch. The catalogue of essays, although less exciting, is worth having

1984   *Furniture, Furnishings: Subject and Object*, Museum of Art, Rhode Island School of Design, New England. The catalogue is an interesting investigation into furniture as metaphor: stimulating and irritating in equal degrees

1985   *Achille Castiglioni*, Pompidou Centre, Paris. An exhibition and catalogue which explores the importance of the 'ready-made' in Castiglioni's design

1985   *De Stijl et l'Architecture en France*, Institut d'Architecture, Paris. Among other things, this exhibition revealed the handicraft construction (and attitude to design) of the De Stijl designers

1985   *High Style: Twentieth-Century American Design*, Whitney Museum of American Art, New York. An excellent catalogue is available; the essays are thoughtful and informative

1986   *Shakers*, Whitney Museum of American Art, New York

1986   *Surface Evidence*, Contemporary Arts Center, Cincinatti, Ohio – major ColorCore exhibition organized as part of an arts/design promotional programme by the Formica Company. Lavish catalogue showing furniture (in post-modernist idiom) by Emilio Ambasz, Milton Glaser, Stanley Tigerman and many others

1986   *Poetry of the Physical*, American Crafts Museum, New York. The catalogue/book accompanying this large exhibition is creamy, excessive and vulgar: it shows handicraft gone to fat, but it documents an important aspect of 1980s American craft-design in furniture

1986   *Vienna 1900*, Museum of Modern Art, New York

1986   *Wohnen von Sinnen* (Living from the Senses), Kunstmuseum, Düsseldorf. An infuriating European exhibition with too many young furniture designers trying to become the Joseph Beuys's of their generation. Thick catalogue of essays and notes

1986   *Architectural League of New York's Chair Fair*, New York International Design Center. This major event gained notoriety because a builder working on site hastily put together a chair made from an up-turned trash can and submitted it anonymously as a send-up of the other exhibits. Inevitably, it won a prize and much praise for its polemic

PUBLICATIONS

Books

Books that have been referred to in the text, or consulted, or which add to or oppose the arguments. All are recommended reading.

Ambasz, E. (ed.) *The International Design Yearbook, 1986/87*, 1986. These Yearbooks are very strong in their coverage of furniture

Banham, R. *Theory and Design in the First Machine Age*, 1960. The definitive account of modernism

Bayley, S., Garner, P., Sudjic, D. *Twentieth-Century Style and Design*, 1986. A well-written survey, with greater concentration on the earlier decades

Baynes, K. & K. *Gordon Russell*, 1980

Bernal, J. D. *The World, the Flesh and the Devil*, 1929, reprinted 1970. A most peculiar piece of futurology which gives the flavour of the excitement that was felt in the early part of this century about machines and science

Branzi, A. *The Hot House: Italian New Wave Design*, 1984

Campbell-Cole, B. and Benton, T. *Tubular Steel Furniture*, 1979

Darling, S. *Chicago furniture: Art, Craft and Industry 1833–1983*, 1984. A scholarly account of furniture as big business

De Fusco, R. *Le Corbusier, Designer of Furniture*, 1979

Garner, P. *Twentieth-Century Furniture*, 1980

Gravagnuolo, B. *Antonia Astori: Designer*, 1983

Green, N. and Donovan M. *The Wood Chair in America*, 1982

Grillo, Paul-Jacques *Form, Function, and Design*, 1975

Hanks, D. *Innovative Furniture in America from 1800 to the Present*, 1981

Hillier, B. *The Style of the Century 1900–1980*, 1983

Jencks, C. *Modern Movements In Architecture*, 1973

Jencks, C. *Symbolic Architecture*, 1985. An important contribution to the understanding of how modern decoration with a comprehensible content can be created

Jencks, C. *What is Post-Modernism?*, 1986

Kouwenhoven, J. *Made in America*, 1948. An exceptionally interesting book which details the rapid development of American engineering and design

Lucie-Smith, E. *Furniture: A Concise History*, 1979

Lyall, S. *Hille: 75 Years of British Furniture*, 1981

Mang, K. *History of Modern Furniture*, 1979

Manzini, E. *The Material of Invention*, 1986. This book shows that Italian design is generating new and practical ideas in every field of consumer product. Again it shows Italy ahead of the design competition

McFadden, D. *Scandinavian Modern Design 1880–1980*, 1983

Meadmore, C. *The Modern Chair, Classics in Production*, 1979

Morello, A. and Ferrieri, A. *Plastiche e Design*, 1984

Naylor, G. *The Bauhaus Reassessed*, 1985. An important book which really does live up to its title

Page, M. *Furniture Designed by Architects*, 1980

Peters, A. *Cabinet Making: the professional approach*, 1984

Pye, D. *The Nature of Design*, 1964

Radice, B. *Memphis: The New International Style*, 1985

Russell, F., Garner, P., Read, J. *A Century of Chair Design*, 1980. Useful, clearly organized and with superb drawings

Sparke, P. *Furniture: Twentieth Century Design*, 1986. Very useful, well-researched book. A good read

Sparke, P. *An Introduction to Design and Culture in the Twentieth Century*, 1986

Stone, M. *Contemporary American Woodworkers*, 1986

Thackara, J. (ed.) *New British Design*, 1986

Venturi, R. *Complexity and Contradiction in Architecture*, 1966

Whitford, F. *The Bauhaus*, 1984

Wilk, C. *Marcel Breuer: Furniture and Interiors*, 1981

Wilk, C. *Thonet: 150 Years of Furniture*, 1980

Wolfe, T. *From Bauhaus to Our House*, 1981

Magazines

A selection of the magazines which offer coverage on contemporary furniture.

Art and Design (UK, monthly)
l'Atelier (France, monthly)
Blueprint (UK, monthly)
Casa Vogue (Italy, 11 times a year)
Crafts Magazine (UK, 6 times a year)
Cree (France, monthly)
Design (UK, monthly)
Designers' Journal (UK, 8 times a year)
DesignWeek (UK, weekly)
domus (Italy, monthly)
Form (Sweden, 8 times a year)
Form and Function (Finland, monthly)
Fusion Design (Japan, monthly)
Das Haus (West Germany, monthly)
Hauser (West Germany, monthly)
Husmorbladet (Norway, 11 times a year)
ID Magazine (USA, 6 times a year)
Interiors (USA, monthly)
Kontur (Sweden, monthly)
Metropolis (USA, monthly)
Mobilia (Denmark, monthly)
Modo (Italy, monthly)
Progressive Architecture (USA, monthly)
Styling (Japan, monthly)

Articles

Brill, M. 'Using Office Design to Increase Productivity', *Progressive Architecture*, January 1985

Britton, A. 'Taking up the chair', *Crafts*, September/October 1985

Buttery, H. 'Thygesen and Sorensen: local heroes', *Designers' Journal*, July 1985

Buttery, H. 'Front row seats', *Designers' Journal*, May 1985

Castle, W. 'Design Considerations', *Fine Woodworking*, Winter 1976

Collins, M. 'The Robert Venturi Collection', *Art and Design*, October 1986

Ellis, C. 'Charlotte Perriand looks back (and forward)', *The Architectural Review*, November 1984

Fawcett, C. 'Shiro Kuramata', *The Architectural Review*, September 1981

Geibel, V. 'Mania for Collecting American Modern', *Metropolis*, October 1986

Glancey, J. 'Furniture by Poltrona Frau', *The Architectural Review*, September 1981

Hemphill, C. 'Against the grain: the art of Wendell Castle', *Town & Country*, May 1984

Jencks, C. 'Symbolic Furniture', *Art and Design*, November 1985

Jencks, C. 'The Corbusier Industry', *Blueprint*, December 1986/January 1987

Knobel, L., Glickman, M., Cooper, R., 'Nomos', *Designers' Journal*, 1987

Leigh Brown, P. 'Is Postmodernism a movement or state of mind?', *Metropolis*, November 1983

Morello, A. 'Salone del mobile e design 1961–1986', *domus*, September 1986

Pawley, M. 'Notes on the bankruptcy of post-modernism', *Crafts*, March/April 1985

Pelli, C. 'The Design Process at Herman Miller', *Design Quarterly*, 98–99, 1975

Romanelli, M., Torricella, A. 'Furniture Design: Knoll International', *domus*, September 1986

Smith, C. R. 'Bürolandschaft U.S.A.', *Progressive Architecture*, May 1968

Smith, C. R. 'The Permissiveness of Supermannerism', *Progressive Architecture*, October 1967

Stone, M. 'Wharton Esherick', *Fine Woodworking*, November/December 1979

Sudjic, D. 'Knoll: a New Gang In Town', *Blueprint*, May 1984

Sudjic, D. 'Who put the art in craft?', *Blueprint*, September 1984

Sudjic, D. 'Milan's New Mood', *Blueprint*, September 1986

ACKNOWLEDGMENTS

Special Acknowledgments

I wish to thank particularly Jasper Morrison; Helen Drutt (of the Helen Drutt Gallery, Philadelphia); Professor Fredrik Wildhagen; Rick Snyderman (of the Snyderman Gallery, Philadelphia); Patrick Johnson; Antonia Astori; the staff at Driade; Anna Castelli Ferrieri of Kartell; Deyan Sudjic and Simon Esterson of *Blueprint* Magazine (who supplied intext pictures by John Barlow on pages 7, 11 and 93); Lance Knobel of *Designers' Journal*; Mark Burns; David Cripps; and Lauri Gibilterra.

I am also grateful to NEOTU; TRIBU; Joyce Clark of Knoll International; Vitra; InterProfil; Herman Miller; Miles-Carter Ltd; Susan Grant Lewin of Formica; Sunar Hauserman; Castelli; Marcatre; Zeev Aram; The Wharton Esherick Museum, Pennsylvania; Gordon Russell Ltd; Thomas Brummett; and all the designers who have supplied material.

Photo Credits

Paul Aoondef 151–3; Aldo Ballo (Driade) 6–8, 13–15, 19–21, 41–5, 76; John Barlow (*Blueprint*) 23, (*Designers' Journal*) 113; Thomas Brummett 143–4, 173, 192; David Caras 187–9; David Cripps 16–17, 157–64; 174–6, 181–3, 221; Jos Fielmich 2–5; Mitsumasa Fujitsuka 40, 63; Hiroyuki Hirai 1, 224; John Kane 185–6; Bruce Miller 196; NEOTU gallery (Paris) 156, 206–8, 215; Boudewijn Neuteboom 68–71; Paul Rocheleau 140; Rick Snyderman Gallery (Philadelphia) 190, 198, 223; Philip Sayer 204; *Stern* Magazine 145, 184; Steven Sloman (Courtesy of Alexander F. Milliken Inc) 193–5; Robert Shackleton 217; Lyn Werner (Sheridan Coakley) 30–1

INDEX